The "Mysteries of the Light"

Sun Gazing for Spiritual Transformation
in the New Age of Light

By

Tom Rees

The "Mysteries of the Light"

"And ye are in great sufferings and great afflictions in your being poured from one into another of different kinds of bodies of the world.

And after all the sufferings ye have struggled of yourselves and fought, having renounced the whole world and all the matter therein; and ye have not left off seeking, until ye found all the mysteries of the kingdom of the Light, which have purified you and made you into refined light, exceedingly purified, and ye have become purified light.

For this cause have I said unto you aforetime: 'Seek, that ye may find.' I have, therefore, said unto you: Ye are to seek after the mysteries of the Light, which purify the body of matter* and make it into refined light exceedingly purified."

*The Soul's subtle embodiment

From the *Pistis Sophia* translated by G.R.S. Mead   pages 207, 208

Dedication

This book is dedicated to those who would let Divine Light illuminate their spirits and Divine Love fill their hearts so they become **"Suns of God."**

My most sincere and loving thanks to my parents, William and Margaret. They sought to know God, but no one could show them how. They devoted their lives to enabling me to follow the whisperings of my Soul.

Preface

We are living at the dawn of the Age of Aquarius. Some say it's the beginning of the Great Year, a 26,000 year cycle. A New Age – an Age of Light – has commenced, accompanied by the manifestation of a New Sun. From the New Sun emanates a New Light – an outpouring of Divine Love and Wisdom.

You can attune to this Light and experience this Divine Love and Wisdom. This Love and Wisdom will transform the nature of your being. Then, you can radiate Divine Love and Wisdom to all around you.

In this New Age, man is evolving towards a higher state of consciousness. **We are slowly transforming from an intellect-based consciousness to a heart-based consciousness.** There is a struggle going on in each person's being – a struggle between one's ego (lower self) and one's Soul (higher Self).

This struggle takes place in the heart. When the heart center is closed, one's self-centered ego is in charge. When the heart center is open, one is in touch with their Soul/higher Self and is guided by the Soul's intelligence, discriminative wisdom, and intuition.

As your consciousness further expands, you begin to experience unity and oneness with your fellows. Rather than seeing others as competitors or enemies – the "us against them" mentality, you'll look at them as your brothers and sisters – "we are all in this together."

Jealousy, selfishness, intolerance, arrogance, and cruelty will be replaced by unconditional love, selflessness, patience, humility, and compassion. Equality, diversity, and inclusion will become the norm. Separateness will dissolve into Unity.

The Divine in me is the same Divine in you. The Light in my eyes is the same Light in your eyes. This Light is the Light of the Soul. We can "awaken" our Souls, allow this Light to shine forth, and become "Suns of God." This book offers a Way.

Table of Contents

Introduction

Throughout history, mystics have used sun gazing as a means of elevating and expanding consciousness and accelerating spiritual evolvement. The *Pythagoreans* and Neoplatonists of Greece, the *Zoroastrians* of Persia, the Judaic sect of the *Essenes*, the *Therapeutae* of Alexandria, Egypt, the *Mithraists* of Rome, the *Hermeticists* of Egypt, the *Brahman* priests of India, the pre-Christian *Gnostics*, and the early Christians are but a few examples.

In past times, the Teachings offered were usually kept secret, preserved by religious orders and brotherhoods dedicated to living The Way of Light. But there are times when they need to be made accessible so those ready to live the Teachings can have access to them, otherwise they could be lost forever.

Now, at the beginning of this New Age of Light, is one of those times. These Teachings are a modernized restoration of the purifying **"Mysteries of the Light."**

Looking at the sun is a perfectly natural thing to do, and it's completely safe **if done in the proper manner with the correct attitude**. Intentionally looking at the sun, often called "sun gazing," has psychological and spiritual effects far transcending physical benefits.

By applying certain sun gazing techniques with the proper attitude and intent, the Light* of the Sun can be used to awaken dormant spiritual faculties and initiate spiritual transformation.**

---

*I use light to represent physical light and Light to indicate light of a higher nature. This will be explained later.

**For our purposes, spiritual transformation is the process by which a human being becomes a spiritual being. In other words, someone identified with their body and personality/ego becomes identified with their Soul, or higher Self. Spiritual refers to matters pertaining to the spirit and does not imply any particular religious connotations.

This book is a practical manual about sun gazing for spiritual transformation. At the core of the process is the purification of the spirit and the opening of the heart center/*chakra*. This is the key to a positive transformation in consciousness. The goal is to experience a state of Unconditional Love and maintain that state so the Light of your Soul can shine forth and you become a "Sun of God."

Sun gazing isn't a religion. <u>It's a spiritual practice that can be used by anyone no matter what their religious belief.</u> Sun gazing is perfect for the aspiring undeclared mystic – one who recognizes the fundamental commonality and unity of all peoples and their religions.

Sun gazing isn't a substitute for meditation. Sun gazing <u>is</u> a passive meditation that attunes you to Divine Love – the true feeling, or nature, of the Soul. Instead of focusing on something, you relax, let go, and allow the Divine Light manifesting through the Solar *Logos* to fill your spirit with Love and Wisdom.

In **Part 1**, I'll begin by offering a few potential benefits from sun gazing, followed by some basic introductory suggestions on how to go about it. Then, I'll discuss attitude, which, though often overlooked, is the **Key** for a successful spiritual transformation.

After that, I present specific sun gazing techniques for purifying the spirit/subtle body and elevating and expanding consciousness. I'll do my best to **clearly** explain the techniques in detail so the sun gazer can practice them successfully. I also include some dietary recommendations and a few comments about sun gazing. **<u>Part 1 is the practical, how-to part of the book. It's the most important part.</u>**

Parts 2-7 are theory and background information. They're an explanation/theory of what's going on during the process of spiritual transformation by sun gazing. It helps to know what you're trying to do, **<u>but you don't need to know everything in order to experience a transformation. Don't be intimated by the technical stuff. Performing the techniques is what brings about a spiritual transformation.</u>**

I think the best way to use this book is to read through **Part 1** and begin practicing the **Attunement-Reflection** T``echnique as soon as you feel comfortable doing so. At the same time you're becoming familiar with the sun gazing techniques, start going through the technical stuff in **Parts 2-7** – a description of the actual process of spiritual transformation.

Of course, it's entirely up to the reader. You could even read **Parts 2-7** independently as an interesting study about the Soul and spiritual transformation without getting into the sun gazing techniques. I believe you'll find what I present to be very informative.

It will probably take some study to grasp the material. Don't expect to fully understand it with one reading. There's a lot of new terminology needing to be explained. **Take your time. Don't get frustrated. And never give up!**

A quick glance at the table of contents will reveal the topics covered in **Parts 2-7**. Subtle anatomy, subtle psychology, and subtle energy dynamics are all relatively new terms. I use the words subtle body and spirit interchangeably. For our purposes, the spirit is the subtle embodiment of the Soul. This will be explained thoroughly.

After I explain the process of spiritual transformation by purification of the subtle body/spirit, I get into the higher states of consciousness that can be experienced by sun gazing. At the end of the book, the techniques are included a second time in condensed form.

Most likely, some who read this book will already be veteran, seasoned sun gazers. There are many different schools of thought on the subject of sun gazing, both past and present. They all have good things to offer. I'm not claiming mine is the only way and others are wrong. Nor do I claim to know everything about sun gazing. I do have almost fifty years of experience.

It depends on your reason for sun gazing. I'm not offering a guide for better health, longevity, or the attainment of super psychic powers, although those might be side benefits. I'm teaching a protocol for spiritual transformation using the Creative Intelligent Life Force manifesting through the sun. I only offer what has worked for me along the Way.

The intent of this book is to inspire a **very** **loosely** connected worldwide Brotherhood of men and women to live these Teachings within their own traditions, use the Light of the Sun for spiritual transformation, and, as living **"Suns of God,"** collectively reflect that Light for the transformation of all of Creation.

Reader's Guide

Often, when you read something in a book, you accept it as true because it's in a book. But that book usually refers to other books which refer to more books, and so on. Anywhere along the line, some author could have accepted something that wasn't true and later authors built upon that untruth.

I've made no attempt to prove what I present in this book with a deluge of references. The only way to prove something is to do it. You have to prove it to yourself. I can suggest a protocol for spiritual transformation and the theory behind the protocol, but I can't experience spiritual transformation for you.

Scientists propose a theory and then perform an experiment in a lab to test the theory. Afterwards, they study the results. Then, others do the same experiment to verify the results. That's the scientific method.

Most of what I talk about is not accepted by modern science because Consciousness, Soul, and spirit cannot be qualified or quantified in the laboratory. For the most part, scientists are confined to the 3-D space time continuum and the electromagnetic radiation spectrum (the limited realm within which their instruments can function), which is only an infinitesimally small portion of ultimate reality.

What I suggest <u>must be experienced</u>. Not litigated intellectually. That's true science. Words cannot adequately describe one's thoughts and feelings to another. I can offer you things to think about and techniques to try, but transformation needs to be lived, not talked about.

As your consciousness elevates and expands – as you open to your higher Self – your intuition will be enhanced. Things will "ring true" to you, or you'll "know" they're false. Until you get to that point, try to keep an open mind.

There's plenty of technical material to immerse yourself in if you're so inclined, But the most important element in spiritual transformation is practicing the techniques and "gettin' the feelin'."

This book is **not** an attempt to patch together a system using ideas from other religions, philosophies or worldviews. I use various schools of thought to explain how sun gazing can initiate a spiritual transformation.

Sun gazing is by no means the only method for spiritual evolvement. It's a tool, like meditation, prayer, fasting, various forms of yoga, and other spiritual practices. When practiced properly, sun gazing can greatly accelerate the elevation and expansion of consciousness.

For the most part, what I present is nothing new. The Teachings I've drawn on have been around for many thousands of years. They are fundamental truths common to all the great religions and philosophies.

My intent is to explain to others how they can experience spiritual transformation by means of God's Divine Light, imbued with His Love and Wisdom, to become living "Suns of God."

Don't be concerned if I don't go into great detail about things early on. I'll get back to them later. The reader might note I repeat myself on occasion. Not all of it's unintentional. Repetition is a good way to stress a point and reinforce memory. I'll try to recap at times to keep the train of thought on track.

On occasion, I use several names for the same thing. Not to cause confusion, but, rather, to link together different systems, or schools, of thought so the reader might be able to identify with things, no matter what their background. I use the / symbol between words to indicate when two or more words have basically the same meaning for our purposes.

Most of the foreign words are *Sanskrit,* from India. The Eastern Masters have a great way of describing spiritual matters. There's no sense in me trying to make up my own terminology. I'm trying to show commonality and universality – not originality. I'll do my best to define my words.

If I say something you disagree with, or conflicts with what you already believe, try to keep an open mind. Try to give what I say some thought and consideration. If I use a word differently than the way you're used to, relax and go with it. At least, for the moment.

It's useless to get into an argument over semantics. I'm trying to explain how sun gazing leads to spiritual transformation – an admittedly open area of research. Talking about it is not the important part. **Doing it is.** I'm sharing techniques I use. **I know they work.**

Although I take spiritual transformation very seriously, I like to approach it with a lighthearted attitude. It helps keep me from getting too full of myself, which only feeds the ego.

Heavy drama contracts consciousness and puts you into an ego-centric state. Joyful laughter diminishes your ego and expands your consciousness.

There's a lot of info in this little book. Straight to the point. I proactively apologize for any typos, misspellings, errors, or confusing trains of thought. Also for the "scintillating" CGI graphics and my lame humor.

Namaste

Part One

Techniques

"The Sons of Light held the highest
reverence for the sun,
but they were not sun worshipers.
They faced the rising sun in the East
and the setting sun in the West,
letting its Light pour through their eyes,
the windows of the soul,
to enlighten their countenances.
Within this Light is God's Love,
which filled their spirits.
Their hearts were wide open to this Love
–the true Agape –
enabling them to experience unity
with God and all of Creation."*

author

*The Sons of Light were a group of *Essene* mystics who withdrew to their desert sanctuary at *Qumran*, near the Dead Sea, to assist in the transformation of the world into Light.

Why Sun Gaze?

The purpose of this book is to explain how to use sun gazing as a means for spiritual transformation. This transformation happens on the subtle level, mostly beyond the physical body. The active agent for this transformation is *Prana* – Creative Intelligent Life Force from the Solar *Logos* which manifests through the sun.

Below, I'll list some reasons for sun gazing. I'll elaborate on these reasons in the following chapters. There's a good chance you haven't heard some of these words. Don't worry about it. You soon will. You're learning a new language about subjects most people don't talk about.

Sun Gazing Can:

Accelerate spiritual evolvement – evolvement of the spirit/subtle body

Awaken dormant and latent spiritual faculties

Expand and elevate consciousness

Dissolve egoity

Energize the Etheric Double

Awaken/energize the *chakras* for better communication between the Soul, the subtle body, the Etheric Double, and the physical body

Awaken *Kundalini*

Purify the astral and mental bodies by breaking up negative *samskaras*

Replace lower, negative thoughts and emotions with higher, positive thoughts and emotions

Put you into a deep meditative state while sun gazing and afterward.

Open the heart center as a channel for Divine Love

Disentangle the mental body from *Kama* and build a "Bridge of Light" between the causal and mental bodies

Shift you from ego consciousness to soul, or super, consciousness

Make you more sensitive to the higher positive vibrations on the astral, mental, causal, *Buddhic*, and *Atmic* planes, enabling you to hear the voices of those who have already traveled the Path

Awaken "you" to your Higher Self

Bring about a transcendental experience. <u>Transcendental</u> literally means climbing above or going beyond. It refers to knowledge beyond ordinary human experience. Knowledge that can't be discovered or understood by ordinary reasoning.

A transcendentalist believes the most important reality is what is sensed intuitively rather than what is thought of as empirical knowledge. **By diminishing egoity and <u>sense-mind</u> consciousness, <u>soul</u> consciousness can be experienced and intuition will guide you.**

Bring about a mystical experience. <u>Mystical</u> means having a spiritual meaning, or reality, beyond the senses and not obvious to the intellect. A mystic believes in the spiritual apprehension of truths beyond the intellect.

He seeks the direct, immediate experience of God in this lifetime (realized eschatology). This results in *Gnosis/* realization of one's own divinity / Self-Realization. One attains insight into ultimate truths leading to spiritual transformation.

No one can have a mystical experience for you. You have to do it yourself. You don't need a priest, minister, or an intercessor. You can experience God and your own divinity by means of His Divine Light – the Spiritual Sun/Solar *Logos*.

Most importantly, by sun gazing, you can utilize the Divine Love and Wisdom manifesting through *Prana* to purify your spirit. Then, the Light of your Soul can shine forth. You become a **"Sun of God"** – reflecting His Light and Love to all Creation and bringing more Divine Love and Wisdom* into the world.

*When I use the word, Wisdom, I'm referring to the Wisdom that will guide us to elevated and expanded states of consciousness – the Wisdom of the Soul.

Note There are numerous psycho-physical benefits from sun gazing. Certain neurochemical and hormonal responses which can <u>alter</u> one's mood, even their <u>state</u> of consciousness, are said to be the result of sun gazing. The pineal gland and pituitary gland are believed to be stimulated. Serotonin production is increased. Vitamin D production is also enhanced.

Some have used sun gazing for healing disease. Longevity is said to be enhanced. Some even say they can live on sunlight alone. That's all great! These effects have been well-documented.

However, I've been unable to <u>directly</u> relate any of these effects to the elevation and expansion of consciousness, which takes place on the <u>subtle</u>, not physical, level.* Altered states of consciousness are **not necessarily** an elevation and expansion of consciousness.

This book is about sun gazing for spiritual transformation which involves *Prana* and *Kundalini* – <u>subtle</u> energies. So, I didn't delve into the psycho-physical effects. I don't deny or discredit these effects. I just don't teach about them in this book.

*Not to say there aren't connections I'm not aware of.

Sun Gazing Basics

Contrary to common belief, you won't go blind if you look at the sun. That is, if you do it in the proper manner. I know people who've been sun gazing for many years and have had no problems. I've been doing it for almost 50 years.

The best times for sun gazing are 15 minutes before sunrise until an hour after and an hour before sunset until 15 minutes after the sun sets. It's also the easiest time because the sun is the least bright then.

This is when the most *Prana* is available. *Prana* is the Creative Intelligent Life Force emanating from the Divine Light of the Solar *Logos*. This force informs and sustains the Universe. *Prana* is also the main force involved with sun gazing for spiritual transformation. (Don't worry! I'll explain this later.)

Experienced sun gazers will probably have no problem looking at the sun. They already have their own way of doing it. I would hope they take a little time to consider the suggestions I'm offering. There are reasons for my method. We're working with *Prana* coming through the sun more than physical sunlight/solar radiation.

Sun gazing can be practiced standing or sitting. Whatever is comfortable. Always stay relaxed. It's important to remain relaxed and open.

When you first start out, a couple of minutes or less of sun gazing at a time is plenty. Unless you can handle a longer time. If you can't hold your gaze for that long, don't get frustrated. As your heart opens up, your eyes will accommodate to the Light. The techniques I offer will make it easier to sun gaze. Take it easy! Work your way up to 10-15 minutes at your own pace.

If the sun is too bright – Stop! If you feel physical pain – Stop! Don't force it. If your eyes are watering and you feel a lot of tension, you're not doing yourself any good. **The whole point is to put yourself into a calm and relaxed deep meditative state WHILE sun gazing. It might take some time to get to this point.** Maybe weeks or months. Don't give up!

Through practice, you'll slowly develop a tolerance as your heart opens and you harmonize with the Light. It's what's in your heart that counts. It's not a matter of seeing how much pain you can stand or showing how tough you are. You're not training for the sun gazing Olympics. You don't have to push through the pain.

If you have trouble getting started, try gazing into the sky for a few minutes before the sun rises or after it sets. You'll still be getting *Prana*.

In fact, you can benefit from sun gazing even with your eyes closed. The Light will still energize and purify your subtle fields and *chakras*/force centers, particularly the "Spiritual Eye"/brow *chakra*.* Most directly involved is your Etheric Double – the subtle energy body that channels *Prana* to vitalize the physical body. (Will be discussed)

When sun gazing, Relax your vision. I never sharply focus my eyes directly on the sun. You don't need to. Let the Light enter your eyes on its own. You don't have to stare it down. I like to gently (without straining) direct my gaze towards the bridge of my nose – in the direction of the "Spiritual Eye." Keep your eyes half open (half mast). No need to be "wide-eyed." This is important! It will make it easier to sun gaze. See pg 127 for details

*I prefer "Spiritual Eye" rather than "3rd eye." No big deal.

Remember: You're not looking at the sun as much as you're looking at its <u>Light</u>, which extends beyond the physical solar orb. In fact, when you look at the sun, you don't really see the physical sun. You see it's light.

I like to keep my gaze moving slowly from right to left and back, up and down, diagonally, or slowly in a circular manner. **Look around the sun more than directly at it.** Full detailed description begins on pg 25.

Just keep your gaze moving around. I find it easier to move my head around a little bit rather than trying to move my eyes around in their sockets. You <u>*don't*</u> have to do this, but over time, I found this to be easier. There's also another reason for this upcoming.

Blinking in a slow, gentle, rhythmic manner is very important. Try to blink every 1-3 seconds or so while sun gazing. It keeps the eyes from focusing on the sun, prevents you from concentrating on one area of the retina, and also keeps your eyes from drying out. Blinking helps you tune into the rhythm of the sun. You'll notice it when it happens. Blinking also helps put you in a relaxed meditative state.

Beginners! *IMPORTANT*: **If you have difficulty facing the sun, try blinking a little faster. As fast as you need to. This will help you get started. <u>Blinking isn't cheating.</u> It will help you open up to the Light. After a time (days, weeks, how ever long it takes), your eyes will gradually accommodate to the sun. <u>Blinking makes it a lot easier to sun gaze. I still blink.</u> Remember: you want to attune to Divine Light. You're not storing up energy like a battery.**

<u>Whenever</u> **you're sun gazing**, it's best to face your open palms to the sun while you're looking at it. You can hold your hands out in front of you (with your arms resting on your sides if you like), let them hang at your sides, or rest them on your knees if you're sitting, all with your palms facing the sun.

The palms have force centers/*chakras*. They allow subtle energy to flow through you. The *Prana*/Creative Intelligent Life Force comes in through your left hand and goes out your right hand after energizing your field. This way you become part of a circuit with the sun and the Light rather than trapping too much energy in your being.

Proper breathing is essential. It's wise to prepare yourself by slowing down your breathing and calming yourself even before you start looking at the sun. Breathe deeply in a relaxed manner to prepare. Then, quietly and softly while sun gazing.

<u>If you're having difficulty getting started, you might try the following techniques:</u>

If the sun is too bright, form imaginary binoculars with your hands and look at the sun through them. This cuts down the glare.

You could try experimenting with different colored cheap sunglasses or colored plastic/cellophane. This will help you get used to sun gazing. Try looking at an image of the sun reflecting off of water in a glass, bowl, pond, even a birdbath. Perhaps, the top of a crystal. Be creative.

As you're facing the sun, try looking at it through the leaves of a tree. This will lessen brightness and glare.

Try holding your open hands (fingers spread with palms facing either outward or toward you) in front of your eyes, crisscrossing the fingers of one hand over the other. Look at the sun through the spaces between your fingers. Try moving your hands back and forth over each other a little bit and observe the effect that creates.

Take advantage of the early morning mist and fog. This cuts down the brightness and glare, making it easier to sun gaze. You'll still get *Prana*.

When you're ready, start out with a couple minutes of sun gazing a day – more or less depending on your tolerance. Gradually increase your sun gazing time. When you're ready for it, 10-15 minutes in the morning and/or 10-15 minutes in evening should be plenty! There's no need to sun gaze more **unless you want to**. **Even 5-10 good minutes a day would be awesome, at first. Slowly work towards it.**

It would be wonderful to sun gaze every day, but for most people it's not really practical or even possible. **Don't stress out!** Do the best you can.

Remember: You're not in a race to enlightenment. You're beginning a process of spiritual transformation that could take months, even years, to experience. After that, you'll want to continue sun gazing for the **enlighten**ment of all of Creation.

Of course, you'll probably want to sun gaze daily. **Try sun gazing on an overcast day. Gaze where you think the sun is. You'll usually be able to see some Light. You'll also get some *Prana*, and you can still feel the Love in your heart. That's what counts!**

Where to sun gaze: It's always better to sun gaze in a tranquil environment like a park, forest preserve, your backyard, an apartment balcony, or out in the country.

If you're "lucky" enough to live in a desert area, make the most of it. In my opinion, there's no better place to look at the sun. It's rarely cloudy, the air is clear, and you get a great view of the sun coming out of the mountains. You can also look at the sun as it rises above the roof of your neighbor's house. **Improvise Adapt Overcome!**

Noise, air pollution, and the hustling and bustling activity of a crowded environment can be a real downer. No one wants a bunch of people staring at them while they're trying to gaze upon the sun. It's best to practice sun gazing in private or with a group of people who are doing the same thing.

However, that's not always possible. You just have to make the best of it. Tune everything else out. Most people won't even notice you, and those who do won't really know, or care, what you're doing. The worst that can happen is they'll think you're crazy. **No** harm in that. Get used to it.

If someone interrupts you, <u>don't get angry or upset.</u> Don't become a sun gazing snob. Sometimes, people just need to talk with someone. Maintain <u>your</u> state of compassion, tolerance, patience, understanding, and Unconditional Love. That's what we're goin' for. That's why we're sun gazing in the first place.

It's good practice, and you'll be helping someone else elevate their state. If that doesn't work, take a break. You can always look at the sun some other time. When it comes to spiritual transformation, you can't rush or force things. Don't go on a sun gazing ego trip! Very counterproductive.

If you're fortunate enough to be able to sun gaze with a group of like-minded individuals, be sure to respect their boundaries. Some sun gazers will want to go around immediately after sun gazing exchanging pleasantries. Others might like to be left alone for a while to reflect on their experience. "Ride their high." Don't take it personally.

Warnings:

<u>**Never**</u> **do anything so utterly ridiculous as looking at the sun with binoculars, a magnifying glass, or a telescope.**

Never try looking at the light of an arc welder. You can/will severely damage your eyes. I don't think gazing at <u>any</u> type of artificial light will do you much good for spiritual transformation because you don't receive *Prana* from artificial light.

Watch out for anger and tension! If you find yourself angry or irritable after sun gazing, **back off**. You're taking in too much energy, and you're not able to handle it. Walking barefoot on the ground can drain off the excess energy. So can standing in water, soaking in a hot-tub, or taking a shower.

Important!!! Sun gazing <u>will</u> amplify your state of being and perception. You **will** be more sensitive to the thoughts and feelings of those around you. If you find yourself getting tense and uncomfortable around others, it might be a good idea to back off sun gazing a little. Perhaps, skip a day or so.

You can also limit the time you spend sun gazing each day. Eating heavier foods will lower your sensitivity. Although it's somewhat counter-productive, it can help if you're really on edge from sun gazing.

Sun gazing <u>will</u> put you into an elevated and expanded state of consciousness. You'll feel it. When you're finished, give yourself a little time (a few minutes) to come down before diving back into "reality."

Be the Love   Feel the Bliss

Attitude is Everything!!!

<u>Always</u> **look at the sun with an open heart full of love.** <u>Never</u> **when you're angry or in a bad mood.** Have no guile, no expectation, no desire, and no demand. Surrender to the Light. Become one with the Light. The idea is to harmonize with the Light and the Divine Love and Wisdom imbued within it.

Remember! You're not seeking super psychic powers or occult ability. Those things happen naturally when you're ready for them – if you need them. Your goal is to experience your Divine Nature. This experience has many names – *Gnosis*, Self-Realization, God-Realization, enlightenment, illumination, *Nirvana* and *Samadhi* are a few.

<u>**Do not**</u> **seek power or control over others**. You're only looking for trouble if you do. With an improper attitude, sun gazing can bring out your dark side. I've seen it happen.

Surrender your self-will and align yourself with Divine Will/*Shakti* (the force behind your spiritual evolution). Then you become an expression of Divine Love on earth. That's the plan.

Feelings of hate, fear, jealousy, arrogance, selfishness, greed, anger, and intolerance close the heart center.

Feelings of love, detachment, selflessness, humility, tolerance, and compassion open the heart center.

<u>NOTHING CLOSES THE HEART LIKE JEALOUSY</u>

Still your mind! Calm your emotions! When you're distracted, you can't open up to the sun and its Light. When thoughts are cluttering your mind and emotions are running through your heart, your consciousness is contracted. When your mind is free of thoughts and your heart harbors no emotions (except Unconditional Love), your consciousness will expand.

You're not trying to <u>project</u> your consciousness anywhere, like another dimension, or plane, of reality. Your goal is to attune to God's Light and Love and reflect them back to the Sun.* Become a mirror. It's an entirely passive act. Don't force it! Let it happen. It's not <u>your</u> will. It's Divine Will.

Don't try to project your consciousness out through your solar plexus. It's entirely <u>counterproductive.</u> This **contracts** your consciousness and closes your heart center, reinforcing the ego consciousness of the sense-bound mind. The whole point of this endeavor is to **expand** your consciousness and open your heart center.

As your consciousness elevates and expands, your egoity is diminished, and you enter into soul consciousness and beyond. You begin to feel a oneness with others, with nature, and with the Divine. You become selfless rather than selfish. <u>s</u>elfless doesn't mean you cease to exist personally. It means you are experiencing your higher Self – the Self which we all share.

There are different qualities of Light at different levels of consciousness. As you elevate to a higher level of consciousness, you'll experience a higher nature of Light and an expanded state of being.

RELAX and BE

*I use the word "sun" to refer to the physical sun and "Sun" to refer to the Spiritual Sun (Solar *Logos*)

Attunement-Reflection Technique

Now, I'll take many of the basics just offered and present them as a good standard technique to work with. There's lots of repetition here, but this will give you an idea of how to put it all together. **I'm not telling you what to do. I'm only sharing what I do.** What I suggest <u>will</u> make it **easier for beginners to sun gaze and experience a deep meditative state. It will also enable you to open up to the Light much quicker.**

<u>**Begin working with this technique as soon as you're ready. Once you become accustomed to sun gazing, I recommend doing this technique for 10-15 minutes, at least once a day, if possible. A few minutes less is okay. So is a few minutes longer. It's entirely up to the individual. The point is to "get the *feelin'*." See pgs 51-54 for details.**</u>

<u>Once a day should be enough. Twice a day is fine as well. It depends on opportunity, time availability, and what you feel like doing. Some people won't feel the need to do it every day. That's fine. Let your intuition guide you. Everybody is different, even though we are all ONE.</u>

This technique can be performed at sunrise <u>and/or</u> sunset, with sunrise being the best time. You can start the technique before the sun comes up. There's lots of good energy already in the sky. And for a few minutes after sunset, too. **It's not really the sun you're looking at – it's the Light.**

You can perform the technique standing or sitting. Just be in a **comfortable** position so you're relaxed. Remember to hold your hands out in front of you, with your palms facing the sun (elbows resting on your sides if you like). You could also let them hang down at your sides or rest them on your knees, if you're sitting down, with your palms facing the sun. This connects you with the Light.

Time for an attitude check. Get into a relaxed meditative state **<u>before</u>** you begin. **Preparation is essential for a successful experience.** It's <u>*very*</u> important to still the mind and calm the emotions for successful sun gazing. I can feel the difference if I try to sun gaze when I'm distracted. It's much harder to face the sun.

Don't be worrying or thinking about anything. Here's your chance to forget about everything. **Let go!** This by itself leads to an elevated and expanded state of consciousness, enabling you to open up to the Light.

I slow down my breathing rate, which in turn slows down the heart rate. You don't need to breathe real deeply – just normally. Don't obsess about it. It's not a breathing exercise. Whatever is comfortable. *The idea is to disengage from body awareness.*

It took some time (years), but I managed to get my breathing rate down to four cycles a minute for sun gazing. That's one cycle every 15 seconds. As a suggestion, slowly inhale for a count of five seconds, hold your breath for three seconds, then slowly exhale for five seconds. Wait two more seconds before beginning the next cycle.

This also slows your heart rate down. **Remember: <u>You don't have to start out this way.</u> It's not essential you do this at all.** Just something you might like to experiment with over time. Slowly work towards it. If you want to breathe less, go for it. As long as it doesn't take a lot of effort. If you want, or need, to breathe more, **please** do.

When sun gazing, do whatever is comfortable. Remember: You're not trying to <u>project</u> your consciousness anywhere. You want to <u>elevate and expand</u> it. This will happen spontaneously. You don't need to focus your mind on anything. Keep your solar plexus relaxed.

Focusing contracts your consciousness. You're really not trying to do anything. It's an entirely passive act. If you relax, you'll **attune** with the Light. It's a natural process. You're surrendering to Divine Will and **reflecting** Divine Love back to the sun. How much effort does a mirror put into reflecting an image? You don't <u>make</u> it happen. You <u>let</u> it happen.

<u>I don't really focus directly on the solar sphere. In fact, I never sharply focus during the entire technique.</u> I **relax** <u>my vision, usually gently aiming my gaze towards the bridge of my nose while at the same time observing the Light within the entire range of my vision.</u> **This will partially close your eyes (about half way), making it easier to sun gaze.**

Your eyes will be slightly out of focus, perhaps even appear a little cross eyed. Don't worry. This won't make you permanently cross eyed. The significance of doing it this way will be explained.   See pg 127.

You hook up the Light of your eyes with the Light of the Sun by just letting it happen. You don't need to zero in on the physical sun.

As I sun gaze, I like to <u>slowly</u> move my gaze around from right to left and back, up and down, as well as diagonally. A few times one way, then the other. No particular order. I move my head slightly rather than moving my eyes. The less eye movement, the better. It's also easier that way.

I also look around the sun in a slow circular manner – either clockwise or counterclockwise, gazing off to the side of the sun and looking all around it, once again moving my head a little bit. **Experiment.**

As I move my gaze around, I blink at a slow rate (1 blink per 1-3 sec). I think this is <u>very</u> important! You can speed up or slow down the rate if you want. It creates an interesting effect. Sync into a rhythm with your gaze motion. <u>Blink faster if you need to.</u>

After you get the basics down, try this: When you begin, both eyes will directly face the sun for a moment. At that time, slowly and gently close your eyes. Then, slowly open them as you slowly move your gaze towards the left until your eyes are open (half mast) and you're right eye is directly facing the sun. **(blink a couple of times along the way if you need to, whenever you need to, while doing the technique)**

It's much easier and more effective if you turn your head slightly. Now, slowly begin closing your eyes again as you move your gaze back towards the sun. Your eyes will be closed again as you directly face the sun.

Then, slowly open your eyes as you slowly move your gaze to the right until your eyes are open (half mast) and the left eye is directly facing the sun. Then slowly move your gaze back towards the sun as you slowly close your eyes again. **Blink more if you want to.** Keep repeating this as long as you want.* **This is a lot easier to do than to talk about.**

The trick is to not focus on the sun. Look at the Light around it. Of course, you'll see the sun. Just don't fixate on it. Easier on the retinas. Keep your gaze movin'. There you go. Get the rhythm.

When looking up and down or diagonally, move your gaze until the sun is almost out of range, then rverse direction. Don't forget to slowly blink. (blink faster if you like) Remember to move your head slightly rather than just your eyeballs. **Remember to keep your eyelids at half mast.**

*Suggestion: 1-3 sec one direction. 1-3 sec back to center. 1-3 sec other direction. 1-3 seconds back to center. Faster or slower if you like, as long as you're not straining.

Once you get a good rhythm going, it's easy. **<u>Basically, whenever your gaze falls directly upon the sun, your eyes are closed for a brief moment</u>**. Don't worry. You're not missing out on anything.

Another thing you can try is holding your gaze directly towards a spot several sun diameters below the sun . Imagine you're aiming the center of your forehead at the sun. Relax your vision and direct your gaze towards the bridge of your nose. Observe the Light rays streaming into your eyes. Or, try looking at a spot several sun diameters above the sun if you like.

Do this for a minute or two. Sometimes, you might see two suns. That's okay, but try to adjust so you only see one. **Don't forget to blink.**

Remember: You're looking for the Light within the light. You'll know what I mean when you see it.

Fellow sun gazers! Don't freak out. It's a lot easier to do this technique than to talk about it. I went into great detail to proactively answer possible questions. Not to make it seem more complicated.

I know it sounds like a lot of stuff going on at the same time. **Once you learn the basic moves**, it's all done without effort. **Don't** get hung up on trying to perfect things. It will slowly happen.

There's no exact routine to memorize. **Don't think about it. Do it. Be spontaneous. Relax. Keep it movin'.** The techniques I'm presenting have evolved over many years. Starting out with these techniques right away should make things much easier for you. *Experiment until you find what works for you.*

One more thing. When performing the Attunement-Reflection Technique, I hold a cross (not a crucifix) in my left palm with the cross facing the sun. My right palm is also facing the sun. This is explained thoroughly on pgs 36-38. **I believe this greatly enhances the effect of the technique. Give it some consideration.**

If using a cross makes you uncomfortable, skip it. Just remember: The cross is a universal symbol. It doesn't link you to any particular religious belief. The cross creates a specific energy pattern/frequency.

Along the way, you'll probably notice your spiritual heart beat. This is the beat that harmonizes with the pulse of the sun. It seems to be about one beat per good slow, solid second. You might've already noticed this beat.

It's a feeling that comes from within in the area of your heart *chakra*/force center. That's the beat I stay in rhythm with. You could call it entrainment. You're linking up to the heartbeat of the sun. You'll be able to distinguish it from your physical heartbeat. Try synchronizing your blinking with it. Don't expect this to happen right away. Someday, you'll just notice it.

Remember! You are responsible for your thoughts and feelings. It's extremely important to keep in mind, when you're looking at the Sun, your thoughts and feelings will be amplified, whether they're positive or negative. Your thoughts and feelings are directly influencing the Sun in a feedback loop. Something to think about. **Don't pollute the Light.**

Reverence, Benevolence, and Gratitude

I think that's an appropriate attitude set. You should be in your highest state – **Unconditional Love** – open to your higher Self. **Be the Love. Feel the Bliss. Realize we are all part of the One.** That's what it's all about, at least, in my opinion.

Recap: First you attune to the Light. This is done naturally/ automatically by letting go which expands and elevates your consciousness. Then you reflect the Light back to the Spiritual Sun. You don't need to do anything intentionally. Don't get hung up in the details. You simply become a mirror reflecting God's Light and Love.

What more splendid thing is there to do?

Performing this technique **will** put you in an elevated and expanded state of consciousness. It's both a transcendental and a mystical experience.

After sun gazing, the ancient mystics went to their abodes and meditated. It's the perfect time. You're at a higher vibrational rate, and your heart center is open. You're already in an elevated and expanded state of consciousness. You don't need to meditate on anything in particular. Get comfortable. **Just Be.**

Close your eyes and gently direct your inner gaze towards the spot at the bridge of your nose. This will direct your consciousness away from the outside world and move it within to the "Spiritual Eye."

Check out what you can "see" with your mind's eye. It's subtle, but you'll definitely notice images. ***Try blinking!*** (with eyes open or closed)You can also lightly press your fingers on your eyeballs and observe various colors and patterns of light.

Suggestion: After you get the hang of the Attunement-Reflection Technique, you might try chanting *Om/Aum* in a slow, pulsating manner for a few minutes ***while*** you sun gaze. This is explained thoroughly in the chapter: *Spiritual Vibrational Healing*, pg 179. No need to do this every time you sun gaze, unless you want to.

It only takes a few minutes. Go through the octave up from middle C, repeating each note several times before going to the next one. See if you notice your force centers resonating. You can concentrate on G – the note associated with the heart center, if you like.

Sun gazing should be an enjoyable and pleasant experience. Don't stress out while you're putting it all together. There's a science behind it, but performing the techniques is an art. It takes time to develop your sun gazing skills.

Just sun gaze in the proper manner with the right attitude. Don't be expecting a change in consciousness. You'll notice it when it happens. **We're using sun gazing to put ourselves into a deep meditative state and an elevated and expanded state of consciousness.** This will be thoroughly explained in the background part of the book. For now, what matters is how you feel during and after performing the technique.

It's important to stay calm and relaxed. Free of negative thoughts and emotions. You'll experience a feeling of Lightness, peace, harmony, Unconditional Love, and ultimately, Bliss. You'll experience a oneness – a unity with all of Creation and the Divine.

Remember to aim your gaze at the spot between your eyes, with your eyes at half mast, and blink at the desired rate.

Once you get the mechanics down, you'll automatically be performing the Attunement-Reflection Technique whenever you sun gaze.

Please note: At the end of the book, I offer a condensed version of the Attunement-Reflection Technique and the other techniques for easier use. You can always refer back to the originals to broaden your perspective. Review sun gazing basics and attitudes.

How Much Should You Sun Gaze?

Earlier, I suggested sun gazing for 10-15 min at least once a day. A few minutes less would be ok, especially to start. Twice a day if you want, time permitting. In my opinion, that would be optimum/maximum for the serious sun gazer seeking spiritual transformation. Once a day should be enough. Sunrise or sunset.

Unfortunately, for most, that's impractical, if not impossible. The demands of everyday life can make it difficult. There's also the weather factor. Don't get discouraged. Much used but useful adage: It's not a sprint. It's a marathon.

I first started sun gazing in the very early 70s, but only on a sporadic basis. Just kinda feelin' it out – "experimentin'." It took me awhile to really get goin'. In the 80s, I sun gazed at least once a week. **It wasn't until late 93 that I began to sun gaze every day for 10 or so minutes at sunrise. That's when things really started happening. Several months later, I started doing sunsets as well when possible.**

Most likely, beginners won't be able to sun gaze for 10 minutes. It will take some time to open up to the sun. That's okay. Don't worry about it. Do the best you can. Just **don't** force it. Let things happen slowly and naturally. Try the suggested techniques if the sun is too bright. Remember: at sunrise and just before sunset, the sun is the least bright. Blink as fast as you need to! Take advantage of the early morning fog and mist.

In the fall of 94, I began to notice I could look at the sun any time of the day, for as long as I wanted. I'm not braggin'. Something just let go. The sun no longer looked harsh and glaring but rather soft and mellow.

That's not the point. You want to get into a deep meditative state **while** sun gazing. You don't need to look at the sun for greatly extended periods of time for that. At least, in my opinion. The important thing is to "get the feelin'"* and enjoy it as long as you can after sun gazing.

*See pgs 52,53

Some intrepid, fearless researchers might want to sun gaze for longer periods of time. Nothing wrong with that. There are no rules etched in stone. Everyone is different. Everyone is in a different situation. I can only share what I do. It's up to each individual sun gazer to decide for themselves.

Watch your attitude. If you find yourself edgy, easily angered, irritable, or quick-tempered, back off for a few days. There is such a thing as being too sensitive or psychic. Too detached from everyday reality or unable to function in society. Unless, of course, you don't care about that.

Don't regard sun gazing lightly. You're taking the creative <u>and</u> destructive forces of the universe into your being. This is serious stuff. These forces are much more powerful than you. I've seen more than one person mess themselves up psychologically by excessive sun gazing. On the other hand, don't be afraid. Just observe good practice and be self analytical. <u>Attitude and intent are extremely important!</u>

Sun gazing **will** put you into an expanded and elevated state of consciousness. The point is to stay in that state as much as possible. Eventually, all of the time. It's what you do the rest of the day, the rest of your life, that really matters. How you live your life. How you treat your fellows. How much Light and Love you bring into the world by being a "Sun of God."

Consider: Make your sun gazing time count. Prepare yourself mentally and emotionally **before** you begin to sun gaze. This will help you "get the feelin'" when you sun gaze. You don't need to sun gaze for long periods to do that. 7-15 min of **"good" (in a relaxed meditative state) sun gazing** is much more beneficial than longer periods of "forced" sun gazing. Of course, more is ok too as long as you stay relaxed and calm.

Don't forget: While sun gazing, relax your vision. Keep your eyes at half mast while gently looking towards the spot between your eyes without straining. Blink rhythmically at the desired rate – the rate that works for you.

Crown Technique

After you become familiar with the Attunement-Reflection Technique – slowing down your breathing, relaxing your vision, gently focusing on the bridge of your nose (the spot on your forehead between your eyes) with your eyes half mast, moving your gaze around, and blinking at the desired rate, all without thinking, you should be really feelin' it.

I realize that sounds like a lot to remember at first. **Don't over think it!** *Relax and let it happen.* Might take a few weeks – maybe longer. Don't worry about it. Everyone has their own time schedule. No need to hurry. Now, you're ready to try the **Crown Technique**.

You're probably already used to holding your palms out while facing the sun. **Important!** You become part of a circuit with the Light. In the palms of your hands, there are *chakras*/force centers that receive and transmit energy/information. You can call this energy/information: *Prana* – Creative Intelligent Life Force. The left hand <u>receives</u> and the right hand <u>transmits</u>. It's a well accepted occult fact.

Performing the technique is very simple. After doing some Attunement-Reflection for a few minutes to get in tune/warmed up, while still holding your left palm outwards facing the sun, take your right palm and place it over the center of the top of your head (the Crown *chakra*), perhaps a quarter inch or half inch above it.

The idea is the Creative Intelligent Life Force coming in through your left hand will radiate outward from your right hand and energize your Crown *chakra*. Continue to sun gaze in the same manner as you do with the Attunement-Reflection Technique while doing the Crown Technique.

I suppose, when you think about it, it might seem pretty silly, just standing there with your hand on top of your head while looking at the sun. **So,** *just don't think about it.* **3-5 minutes** should be long enough, but feel free to go longer if you like.

If your right arm gets tired, just lower it for a moment or two to loosen up and then place it back over your head. You can do this several times if you need to. This is not a strength or endurance contest. It's important to stay comfortable and relaxed. You don't want to be thinking about your sore arm. You want your thoughts and feelings to remain calm. If you're sitting down in a lawn chair, you could at least rest your left elbow on the chair.

There's one important embellishment you can/<u>should</u> add to this technique. It's the KEY to the whole technique. Place a cross (not a crucifix) with a chain or cord on the center of the palm of your left hand. It's not critical which side is facing out. Whatever feels right to you.

Take the chain or cord of the cross and place it through the crotch between your middle finger and your ring finger, with the cross laying in the center of your palm. Then, wrap the chain or cord around and/or between your fingers so it will hold the cross in place. No special way to wrap the chain – just whatever works for you.

There are many styles of crosses. A basic, simple one should work fine. It's okay to get fancier. Originally, I used a version of an ancient *Nestorian* cross. Celtic solar crosses look like they'd be fine as well. A crucifix is not really necessary or appropriate, but it's ok if you want to use one. (Perhaps, that's all you have)

The cross I used to use was rather big – 3 inches by 2 inches. Recently, I've been using a Celtic Solar Cross <u>pendant</u> one and a quarter inches in diameter. Both seem to work fine. Awesome Light and a great feeling. Any size in between should work.

Some crosses have a long vertical element and a shorter horizontal arm. Others have arms all the same size. I've seen some really nice <u>Celtic Solar Cross Pendants</u> with equal length arms online (inexpensive; I have/use one now). <u>They look just like the symbol of the Solar *Logos* (below) without the sunburst of rays projecting from it.</u> Might be worth a try. Whatever speaks to you.

A simple cross will do – doesn't have to be expensive. I used a silver cross. Gold's too expensive for me. Now, I use a pewter cross. Shouldn't really matter. In a pinch, one could take a good-sized nail clipper and slip some tweezers through it at a 90° angle to make a cross and hang it from a piece of dental floss (that's what MacGyver would do).

What counts is the shape of the cross, which is a symbol – a symbol of the *Logos*. A symbol creates a particular energy field. So, by placing a cross in the palm of your left hand and facing it towards the sun, you are tuning to a specific frequency – the frequency of the Solar *Logos*. The frequency of Divine Love. (If you don't have a cross, imagine one.)

Symbol of the *Logos*

This specifically tuned energy will flow through your field and pour out through your right hand, which is being held slightly over the top of your head in the area of your Crown *chakra*. You **could** say you're anointing your Crown *chakra* with the Solar *Logos* because **that's what you're doing**.*

*Could be why some mystics/priests drew symbols on their palms.

This technique worked for me – still does. **In fact, whenever I sun gaze, whether I'm doing the Crown Technique or not, I use the cross in my left hand. I can notice a difference in the Light when I use the cross.** You can also do this technique over your heart *chakra*, "Spiritual Eye", or whatever other *chakra* you want. I believe the Crown and the heart are the most important – they work together.

This should get you started. I offer a detailed explanation of how this works later. See pgs 143-146.

Important! **As you perform the Crown Technique, continue doing the basic Attunement-Reflection procedure – moving your gaze around while blinking in a slow rhythmic beat and gently directing your gaze to the spot between your eyes with your eyes at half mast.**

When you finish with the Crown Technique, continue doing the Attunement-Reflection Technique for a while longer if you like. Maybe, place your right hand over your heart *chakra* for a few minutes.

Consider the Attunement-Reflection Technique as the standard go-to sun gazing technique whenever you sun gaze. Augment it with the Crown Technique. I recommend performing the Crown Technique once a day for 3-5 minutes, if possible. Longer if you like.

Note: I don't think the cross necessarily has to be metal. It's the symbol that counts, like in radionics. I use a metal cross because that's what I have. We're using the cross as a symbol, not a talisman or a religious artifact. More research needs to be done in this area. Try a metal cross for a few weeks or months and then try one of wood or some other material. See if you can tell/feel the difference. **In a pinch, try drawing the Solar *Logos* symbol on the palm of your left hand. (Rays optional)**

Heart Center Technique

The Soul expresses itself through the heart center. This is the center from which you radiate Unconditional Love.

After performing the Attunement-Reflection Technique for a few minutes with your cross in your left hand facing the sun, place your right hand over your heart *chakra,* about a quarter inch away from your body.

Remember to continue sun gazing in the previously prescribed manner. This technique will attune the heart center with the expression, or feeling, of the Solar *Logos* – Divine Love.

Concentrate your awareness on the heart center as you perform the technique. Feel the love pouring into you and filling your entire being.

After a time, a few minutes or more, take your right palm and face it towards the sun, with your left hand and cross still facing the sun. This will close the circuit with the Spiritual Sun/Solar *Logos*.

Feel the love radiating to everyone and everything. You have an endless supply of Divine Love because it's your true nature.

Experience Unity with all of Creation and the Creator. Be the Love. Feel the Bliss. When you feel these qualities, you radiate them outwards spontaneously. You become a channel of Divine Love.

You can make it a meditation, if you like. Envision Divine Love emanating from you and surrounding and enveloping everything and everyone around you. You **are** the Light* (imbued with Divine Love), so <u>Be</u> the Light.

It doesn't need to be sunny. You can perform this technique when it's overcast. Just gaze where you think the sun is and go for it. You'll probably be able to see <u>some</u> Light. Perhaps, of a soft golden hue. Notice the warmth in your heart center.

*You are a Soul – a Ray of Divine Light

The proper attitude is reverence, which is love for the Divine and benevolence, which is love for your fellows.

You're in a detached state – detached from thoughts and emotions. No mindless chatter in your head. No roiled emotions in your heart. No pulls or attachments.

You're not disturbed by events going on around you. You're not attached to desires. You harbor no desire, no guile, no demand, and no expectation.

You're centered in your heart *chakra* – the center of your being.

Make sure your solar plexus is relaxed

Listen only to the silence of your Soul

You're calm, peaceful, and serene. At one with everything and everyone. You're in your highest state – **Unconditional Love**.

After you finish with the Heart Center Technique, continue with the Attunement-Reflection Technique for a while longer if you wish.

Remember: Manifesting through the sun, along with physical light, is Divine Light imbued with Divine Love. You experience this Light and Love in proportion to how much you're attuned to It. The more your heart center is open, the more you receive and radiate Divine Light and Love. Open your heart by surrendering to the Light.

Spirit Cleansing Technique

As you begin to become more Self-aware, you'll learn to recognize any negative thoughts or feelings. Watch out for any attitude that's counter productive to your spiritual evolvement – the elevation and expansion of your consciousness.

Simply put, any thought or feeling that closes the heart center. That's where you feel it – a twingy (twinjee) sensation in the area of the heart center. You'll feel spiritually "unclean." Nothing worse than an **<u>unclean</u>** spirit. **Nasty!**

Any selfish, hateful, angry, jealous, intolerant, or other negative thought/emotion will close your heart center and contract your consciousness. This will prevent you from opening up to the Light. **Very counterproductive!**

These negative thought-emotion forms are vibrating energy patterns in your spirit/subtle body (mental and astral bodies). They're transmitted through the Etheric Double and create fixed patterns of tension in the soft tissues of the physical body. That's technical enough for now. At least, for me.

There are many ways to break up the negative vibes stored in your body and psyche. Exercise can burn up these patterns, as can massage. Meditation can do it as well. Here's an amazin' little technique I stumbled upon out of sheer necessity:

I found little splashes of cold water can shock the soft tissues and break up these patterns. The shock sends impulses through the nerves, which are then transmitted to the centers of sensation in the astral body by *Prana.* This interrupts the reflex arc.

The net result is the negative energy patterns are broken up, and the spirit, at least to some extent, is cleansed. That's my theory. I just know it works because I can feel it.

Try this sometime, preferably on a sunny day:

Sit down on a chair, bench, boulder, log, or some steps, with your bare feet on a flat rock, concrete, sand, or some grass. This will ground you. Plain dirt might get a little muddy. You can glance up at the sun occasionally while you perform this technique.

Take a little time. Relax. Get into it. Pour a small amount (an ounce) of **cold** (more shock value) water over each foot. Wait a few seconds and do it again. Wait a moment and do it one more time for a total of 3x. Feel the negativity wash away. Use more water if you want.

Next, pour a little cold water in your hands and rinse them a bit –a total of three times. (especially the backs of your hands) Pause briefly between each wash. Don't rush things. Savor the experience. Observe how you feel. You don't need a whole lot of water. Remember: you're not bathing. **The initial shock does the job.**

After that, pour a little cold water on your fingertips and splash/ rub it on your forehead – 3 times of course. Just a few drops.

Do the same thing to the nape of your neck. Just a few drops, once again, 3 times.

Finally, to the top of your sternum, if you care to. Yeah, 3x, just a few drops.

You'll probably feel more relaxed now – more centered. Your breathing will be deeper. You'll be more open to the Light. **Clean!**

Take an inventory of your thoughts and emotions. See if you still feel any negativity. Hopefully, you won't. At least, for a while.

If you have any sacred stones or a cross you use during sun gazing, you can rinse them 3x and hold them up to the sun to purify them. You might even notice the Light of the Sun will now seem more pure.

No need to do this technique every day. Only when you feel like you need to. Think of it as a quick tuneup. (a cold shower will also work)

Sun Gazing as Meditation

I suggest sun gazing, when done in the proper manner with the correct attitude, is a form of deep meditation. Allow me to explain.

A basic recommendation for most types of meditation is to sit in a relaxed position (not necessarily a full lotus). The obvious difference is in sun gazing most people stand. However, you can sit in a comfortable position while sun gazing. (I do) You can also stand in a relaxed, comfortable position.

Another preliminary for standard meditation is slowing your breathing rate. Same thing for sun gazin'. You're also instructed to calm your thoughts and emotions, just like in sun gazing. This in itself elevates and expands your consciousness – the purpose of meditation.

It's extremely important to be emotionally and mentally in a relaxed state while sun gazing and/or meditating.

Often, in meditation, one chants *OM* to put oneself in harmony with the rhythm of the universe. You can do the same thing while sun gazing.

Sometimes, in meditation, you gaze upon or visualize a certain image. In sun gazing, you gaze at the Light. Both acts attune you to a certain frequency.

Sometimes, in standard meditation, you just let your mind go blank – free to wander. Same as in sun gazing. In fact, that's one of the keys to successful sun gazing – just letting your self go. (Spiritual pun)

In *kriya* yoga meditation, the aspirant is asked to gently fix his gaze on the point at the bridge of his nose. Just like the way I suggest when sun gazing. Both acts help you shift from body consciousness to soul consciousness. There's more to this comin' up in a bit.

The purpose of spiritual meditation is to calm down your personality (lower self) and put it under the control of the Soul (higher Self). Shift from ego consciousness to soul consciousness. Isn't that the purpose of sun gazing? Answer: Yes!

Deep meditation and sun gazing have the same goal: spiritual awakening – enlightenment – illumination – Self-Realization – *Gnosis*.

Meditation can give you a transcendental and\or mystical experience. So can sun gazing.

During meditation, just like in sun gazing, you can experience Oneness – unity with your fellows and the Divine. In both spiritual practices, you must relax and go within to a higher state of consciousness.

Meditation can burn up *samskaras*. So does sun gazing.

Meditation and visualization are often used to energize the force centers and awaken *Kundalini*. **Sun gazing in the proper manner with the correct attitude does this too.**

Both practices enhance communication between the Soul and the personality by widening the channel/connection between Lower and Upper *Manas* in the mental and causal bodies. This channel is called the *antahkarana*, or "Bridge of Light." (more on this later)

Both practices put one in Harmony with Divine Love and Wisdom emanating from the Solar *Logos*/Spiritual Sun.

Sun gazing and meditation both calm down the thoughts and emotions in your subtle body so it can be reprogrammed with higher vibrations of Divine Love.

Meditation and sun gazing can elevate you to *Buddhic* consciousness, where you experience unity with your fellows and the Divine and eventually to *Nirvanic* consciousness, where you experience non-duality. You realize you are, in essence, Divine. For our purposes, realize means to experience.

So, it would seem meditation and sun gazing are not only similar in the way they are practiced, but they achieve the same goal. **Therefore, I suggest sun gazing is a form of meditation – deep, intense meditation. At least, the way I recommend sun gazing.**

I'm not proposing sun gazing should be a replacement for standard meditation. In fact, I believe they can go hand-in-hand. After sun gazing, take a little time, go indoors maybe, and do some standard meditation with your gaze fixed on that area between your eyes, whether they're closed or not. This not only extends your heightened state of consciousness. It can make it more permanent.

I firmly believe, when done in a proper manner with the correct attitude, sun gazing can bring about a spiritual transformation much quicker than meditation alone. What might take years of serious meditation practice can be accomplished in months by sun gazing properly. Maybe less, depending on your level of evolvement. **That's the purpose of this book.**

Like meditation, sun gazing should be continued for the rest of your life to maintain your state of soul consciousness and beyond. Become a Living "Sun of God," shining Divine Light, Love, and Wisdom* on all of Creation.

*We're talking about the Wisdom of the Soul. The Wisdom that guides you on your path of spiritual evolution.

Dietary Suggestions

Although I'm presenting a system for <u>spiritual</u> regeneration and transformation by sun gazing, I'd be remiss if I didn't offer a few dietary suggestions.

I know some people sun gaze to heal diseases. Some are even trying to condition themselves to live on sunlight. I think that's awesome. I admire those who try, and I wish them well. I might try something like that when I'm ready to leave this plane. But that's **not** what I'm teaching.

I would imagine most people attracted to sun gazing are already somewhat conscious of their diet. I strongly discourage eating meat such as beef and pork, which I quit eating in the mid-80s. Aside from the moral reasons, these meats are heavier, harder to digest, and clog the lymphatic system with partially digested protein particles, which can lead to disease.

Not to mention the chemical additives. Meat also dramatically lowers your vibrational rate and your level of consciousness, dulls your receptivity to higher vibrations, and affects your personality.

I continued eating turkey and chicken for a long time while sun gazing. Fish is also lighter. Eventually, I totally lost my taste for all animal flesh. I didn't like the thought of killing something to eat it, nor did I want someone else to carry that karma for me. You'll probably feel that way eventually, as you become more sensitive to the vibrations of our animal friends.

A quick study of vegan and plant-based diets shows a lot of gray area and overlap between the two, depending on which website you look at. No use getting into that. It's not my field of knowledge. They're all better than the traditional meat and potatoes Western diet.

Some discourage the use of eggs because you're killing the embryo. Dairy products such as yogurt, milk, butter and cheese aren't harmful to the animal. I lost my taste for eggs, but I'm sure eggs are used in some foods I eat – particularly bakery products. I eat a little cheese and yogurt. (Maybe, a little? bit of ice cream) I don't claim to eat the perfect diet.

A diet of fresh vegetables, grains, fruit, and nuts, throw in a few sprouts, and you have a winner. If you can live on it. Talented raw food chefs can really make some awesome creations, but a totally raw food diet isn't for everybody and it's a lot of work. Sprouted bread is awesome.

A little common sense doesn't hurt. Never eat a heavy meal just before sun gazing. You won't be able to stop thinking about your stomach. In fact, it's never really good to eat a heavy meal. It's better to have multiple smaller meals during the course of the day. The simple fact is most people overeat. If you like to fast, you're already on your way to higher consciousness!

If you're already a raw food advocate, or live only on nuts and berries, that's awesome. If you're a purist who subsists on *Essene* sprouted bread, "good on ya." If you avoid heavy meats and go easy on the lighter meats and fish, you should be okay. At least, to start with. Don't get too hung up on your diet or turn into a food purist snob. You'll become all about your diet. That can puff up the ego.

The point I'm trying to make is you don't have to be a fanatic, in my opinion. **At least, not at first.** Over time, you'll hopefully slip into good dietary habits. It's up to each sun gazer to decide for themselves. You'll know what works for you. **The main thing is:**

Don't let your concerns over diet prevent you from sun gazing.

Remember: sun gazing for spiritual transformation is a lifelong process. There will be plenty of time to adjust your diet as you go along. **The key is to practice the techniques as much as possible. Don't link their practice to lots of other lifestyle changes.** If you try to make too many changes at one time, you'll make it a lot harder on yourself.

In my opinion, alcohol is a nonstarter. Not only does it make you more emotional, cause you to be melancholy and morose, impair your judgment, and dull your senses. It seriously lowers your vibrational rate. It also makes you more susceptible to negative psychic influence.

Alcohol seriously traumatizes your Etheric Double – the medium for exchange of incoming and outgoing energies/vibrations between the subtle body and the physical body How can you elevate and expand your consciousness when you're trying to make yourself **un**conscious?

Things started happening fast for me when I quit drinking in late 92 and began sun gazing seriously in 93. How about the occasional glass of wine at dinner or an ice cold beer on a hot summer day? Just to relax? That's up to you. **Never** drink right before or right after sun gazing. If you do, you're asking for trouble and you're wasting your sun gazing efforts.

Pay attention to how you feel after a drink and then after another drink, etc. That should answer the question for you. I would think, after a while, you'll probably feel too good from sun gazing to want to drink. Nothin' better than a **clear** head. Why ruin the sun gazin' "high"?

Coffee and cigarettes are another issue. Aside from health issues, coffee can get you wired up and make it hard to relax while sun gazing. Course, some people need a cup of coffee to get themselves goin' in the morning. No big deal. Nicotine is a **serious** toxin that can harm not only the physical body but the Etheric Double as well. None of this is really news. Everything in moderation. It's up to you.

Along the way, you might want to go on a detoxification/ rejuvenation regime for a period. This alone can elevate your consciousness. You'll be more sensitive to the higher vibrations from the astral, mental, causal and higher planes and less responsive to the lower vibrations. Ultimately, this is what you're after.

It's also good preparation if you're considering altering your diet or dramatically reducing your food intake. Over the years, I've done quite a few cleansing regimes. Always feel better afterward.

The Etheric Double – the interface between the physical body and the subtle body – sometimes called the body of *Prana*, is particularly affected by a physical body that's coarse, dense, thick, and dull. Remember: vibrations from the Soul have to go through the Etheric Double to affect the brain.

When you purify the physical body, you're also purifying the Etheric Double. By "lightening" your physical body and Etheric Double, you'll be much more responsive to the higher positive vibrations of Love and Wisdom.

I'm not giving you medical advice. Just sharing some things with you that worked well for me. There are plenty of cleanses and rejuvenation regimes out there. You should be able to find something that works for you.

Consult a natural healthcare practitioner for guidance. The older you are, the more careful you need to be. Once again, **none of this is mandatory for sun gazing for spiritual transformation, but it could be of great benefit to you, both physically and spiritually.**

Sun Gazing Reflections

The main objective in sun gazing for spiritual transformation is to shift from ego consciousness to soul consciousness and higher states. This will be explained in great detail in the upcoming chapters.

Fortunately, you don't need to know all the background teachings to have a successful sun gazing experience. Practicing the techniques in the proper manner with the correct attitude will take you a long way.

Some people reading this book are already seasoned sun gazers. Others may have never tried it before. I think even beginners will be able to gaze at the sun as it first comes above the horizon and just before it sets. Following the recommendations **will** make it easier to sun gaze.

If you have difficulty, try the binoculars technique or the crisscrossing technique. They both cut down on the glare, making it easier to sun gaze. So does looking through the leaves on a tree.

Try sun gazing on a hazy or overcast day. This can make it easier. Remember to blink rhythmically while moving your gaze around the sun rather than directly at it. It might take some time, but eventually, you'll open up to the sun. It took me a while to get goin'. Everyone is different.

The most important thing while sun gazing is to **RELAX. To enter into a deep meditative state.** If your eyes are watering, your nose is running, and you're writhing in agony, you won't be able to get into the necessary calm meditative state which is the key to the whole process. We want to detach from body awareness. Not painfully immerse ourselves in it.

Don't forget to keep your eye lids at half mast, gently direct your gaze towards the spot at the bridge or tip of your nose, and relax your vision. Just let go. Don't try to focus. Your eyes might almost seem a little crossed. Don't be concerned. It won't be permanent. This makes it much easier to look at the Light around the sun without straining. Don't forget to blink at a comfortable rate. You can slow down the blinking as you accommodate to the Light.

It's very important to be "in the now" while sun gazing. If you're thinking about what you're going to do later on, what you're going to have for lunch, or about some problem messing up your life, you won't be able to open up to the Light.

On occasion, I've attempted to sun gaze while distracted. I couldn't look at the sun. It appeared too bright. Too harsh. But when I let everything else go, stilled my mind, and calmed my emotions, the Light became soft. Easy to look at. You might even try meditating for a few minutes beforehand to get into the right mood.

Once you settle in and get comfortable with sun gazing, the Attunement-Reflection Technique will put you in a deep meditative state. In fact, many elements of sun gazing are exactly the same as meditation. In both practices, you work yourself into a calm and relaxed state by slowing your breath rate and letting go of thoughts and emotions.

This alone puts you in a higher state of consciousness. Rather than concentrating on a mantra or an image, you gaze around the sun, allowing Divine Light imbued with Love and Wisdom to flood your being.

You harmonize with those vibrations – attuning to them thus elevating your own frequency. It's a passive act. This Love and Wisdom will open your heart center, moving you into higher states of consciousness. **This is what brings about a spiritual transformation!**

When you tune into the Light, you're in heightened state of awareness. You feel "high." No better way to describe it. You're "kicked back." Time seems to stop. It feels like "you" have stepped outside of "your self." It's an "out of your body experience." You no longer identify with your body. "You" is who's looking out through some eyes. At some point, you'll say **WOW!**

You might feel a oneness with everyone and everything around you. You might feel a oneness with all of Creation. You might feel a oneness with the Light. You might feel a oneness with the Divine. That's our ultimate goal. This is called Absolute Unitary Being (AUB).

Peace Bliss Joy Contentment

You feel light – detached from your body. You just <u>ARE</u>. No thoughts or emotions except Unconditional Love. You might find it difficult to talk for a few minutes afterwards. You might not want, or even be able, to talk for a while. You have no thoughts or desires. You just want to savor this expanded state. You realize you're an immortal soul.

The protocol I suggest is a simple, streamlined way to put you into soul consciousness and higher. At least, while you're performing the Attunement-Reflection Technique. As time goes on, you'll be able to maintain that state for a longer time, eventually remaining in soul consciousness, or super consciousness, and beyond all the time.

Don't expect this to happen after 10 minutes of sun gazing. It could take weeks or months. What's the rush? You'll be sun gazing for the rest of your life. **<u>If you continue to practice the techniques in the proper manner with the correct attitude and intent, something will happen. You will notice a change in yourself.</u>**

Every time you go into soul consciousness, you're slowly changing/reprogramming your spirit – the mental and astral bodies (will be explained). By entering this higher state of consciousness, even for a while, you're purifying your spirit.

That's why it's important to do the techniques on a regular basis. Once every day would be optimal. Twice a day if you're so inclined. Of course, that's usually not possible. And probably not necessary.

Weather <u>can</u> make it difficult. So can worldly responsibilities like school, a family, or a job. **<u>Don't panic!</u>** Remember the heart center technique and the spiritual vibrational healing technique (pg 179), as well as any other spiritual practices you might have that can elevate and expand your consciousness on a cold, cloudy day.

What you do between sun gazing sessions is just as important as sun gazing. <u>Learn to become aware of your thoughts and feelings.</u> **Pay attention!** When you find yourself thinking a negative thought or harboring a negative emotion, stop and **get a grip on your trip**. Replace negative thoughts and negative emotions with positive ones.

This is important. This will help you break away from your previous mental and emotional conditioning. This happens when you heal yourself with Divine Love. I should say, when you <u>let</u> Divine Love heal you. **The positive vibrations experienced while sun gazing will reprogram you.**

The more you experience soul consciousness, the more you'll be guided by your intuition. You'll hear your inner voice of discriminative wisdom – you'll know instinctively what's right and what's wrong, what's true and what's false. Pay attention to that voice.

Cultivate unconditional love, selflessness, compassion, kindness, and sympathy. Watch out for sudden impulses or desires. Don't respond to them. Pay attention to how you treat your fellows.

Be Aware

Be patient. Don't expect instantaneous results. Don't expect an immediate spiritual transformation. Don't expect <u>anything</u>. Enjoy the techniques for what they are. Get into the sun gazing experience – the natural high, the peace, and the Bliss. Transformation will come in time, depending on your level of evolvement – how far along you are on your path. Sun gazing <u>will</u> accelerate the process.

Note: It would be impossible for me to anticipate every question about practicing the techniques that may arise. **Questions and comments are encouraged. Don't hesitate.** I'm not gonna ask for money. You don't have to join my club (I don't have one). My mission is to teach sun gazing for spiritual transformation to those who want to do it.

Email: photismos1994@gmail.com

Part II

Origins and Forces

"If they say to you, 'Where did you come from?'
say to them,
'We came from the light, the place
where the light came into being
on its own accord and established
[itself] and became manifest
through their image.'"

Logion 50 of The Gospel of Thomas   from the *Nag Hamahdi Library*

Origin and Organization
of the Universe

Almost every culture and religion has its own story of creation and the origin of man. How can there be so many different stories? Because they're myths – stories to explain an unknowable or inexplicable event. Myths are not meant to be taken literally.

Not to imply they're wrong. They're constructed to convey a teaching. They're different viewpoints of the same story within various cultural contexts. These myths are the foundation of almost every faith/based belief system.

What I offer in the next couple of pages is more of a description of the nature of the Universe and the Soul rather than exactly how they came about. Admittedly, it's my own interpretation, but it's an interpretation based on some very ancient teachings. Note: I'm not excluding the possibility of past and future universes or simultaneously occurring multi-verses. One universe at a time is enough for me.

There's no need to abandon your own religious beliefs. I'm just offering background for the work we're going to undertake – the purification of the spirit and the "awakening of the Soul." **If these first few pages seem a little heavy, don't worry about it.** It gets easier.

Absolute Spirit (Consciousness) is Transcendent God <u>beyond</u> vibratory Creation. Emanating from Absolute Spirit (Consciousness) is Imminent God <u>in</u> vibratory Creation, sometimes called the *Logos* or "Word of God." "In the beginning was the Word."

The *Logos* (sometimes called the Solar *Logos*) can also be considered as the Spiritual Sun, or God's firstborn. God said: "Let there be Light." **Everything in the Universe is some form or condition of that Light – the Light of the Solar *Logos*.**

Consciousness, as Divine Light – the Solar *Logos*, is a threefold manifestation. First, Consciousness becomes primordial "matter" (vibratory energy patterns of different frequencies)– the material making up the planes, or realms, of nature for Consciousness to manifest.

Then, Consciousness, as Creative Intelligence, organizes the material into various stratified planes of different vibrational rates for Consciousness to manifest. The active agent for this is *Prana* – Creative Intelligent Life Force. *Prana* is also the guiding intelligence and force that creates and sustains the vehicles/bodies of the Soul, including the physical body, for pure Consciousness to "descend into matter."

Finally, pure Consciousness, Itself, differentiates into individual-ized Souls that "descend" into the various planes of Consciousness. Put another way, the Solar *Logos* creates "matter," then organizes the "matter" into planes and vehicles through which the Soul (individualized Consciousness) can interact with vibratory Creation. This is how God becomes the entire Creation, including us. **<u>Everything</u> is a manifestation of Absolute Spirit/Consciousness.**

There are seven planes of Consciousness in Nature. The first is called the *Logoic* (*Logos*) plane. The next, the *Monadic* plane, is followed by the *Nirvanic*/*Atmic*, *Buddhic*, Mental, Astral, and finally the Physical planes. As well as a state, or condition, of Consciousness, each plane is a realm of "matter," or dimension.

The planes vary in density – each plane consisting of matter of a particular range of vibrations, starting at an inconceivable rate in the *Logoic* plane, then becoming slower and denser until finally reaching the physical plane of which we are most commonly aware. Through these planes, Consciousness "descends" from the *Logoic* plane into the "physical" plane as the Soul.

The matter of each plane exists in seven grades (sub-planes), or orders, of vibration, with the finest matter in the first sub-plane and the coarsest in the seventh. The different degrees of density of the matter of which they are composed are determined by their vibrational rates/ frequencies, not their physical condition or particular location.

So, there are seven planes of Consciousness/Nature, each with seven sub-planes, for a total of 49 sub-planes differentiating, or unfolding, from the *Logos*. (Not too critical for our work)

It's important to note these planes are not separate, distinct layers. The planes, or realms of nature, are not separated in space. They interpenetrate each other, all existing simultaneously, though in different dimensions (different ranges of vibrations/frequencies).

These planes are not places. You don't need to go anywhere or project your consciousness* somewhere to experience these planes. Because they exist in nature outside of our normal perceptions, we only need to develop the senses, or faculties, to perceive these planes. This is done by elevating and expanding your consciousness.**

*You, a Soul – an individual unit of Consciousness – already exist on these planes. You're just not aware of this, **yet**.

**To differentiate between Consciousness/Absolute Spirit/God and one's conscious awareness, or state of consciousness, I'll capitalize the former and use the lower case c for the latter.

Origin of the Soul

Now, specifically for the origin of the Soul. Absolute Spirit, Consciousness transcendent <u>beyond</u> Creation, wills Itself into manifestation and becomes the *Logos* (the Word) – Consciousness imminent <u>in</u> Creation. On the *Monadic* plane, the *Logos* differentiates into units of Consciousness which can be considered as rays of the *Logos*.

On the *Nirvanic/Atmic* plane, these units of Consciousness/Spirit exist in a state of non-duality before finally emerging as individualized Souls (still in unity) on the *Buddhic/*Christ plane. From there, Souls descend into the causal plane* as <u>individual</u> human Souls where they remain and work through the mental, astral, and physical bodies to interact with the physical world. Remember: These planes are not spatial realms but levels of consciousness.

From another perspective, Consciousness, manifesting as the Solar *Logos*, is Divine Light. From the *Monadic* plane, Rays of this Divine Light emerge as Souls in the lower planes. The Soul **is** that Divine Light and Consciousness <u>in</u> your body. You are a Soul. The Soul <u>is</u> the "real" you. You are a ray of Divine Light.

.

In some schools of thought, Self is considered God. Everything is a manifestation of the Self. The higher Self could be called the *Monad*, the Ego, or the Soul, depending on which plane you're referring to. To simplify matters, I will refer to the higher Self as the Soul <u>most</u> of the time. Remember: **We are all immortal Souls**. Actually, we are all **One** immortal Soul.

For our purposes, evolution of the Soul is specifically the evolution of the causal and subtle bodies so the Soul can better work through them. That's what reincarnation is all about.

*The 3 highest sub-planes of the mental plane make up the causal plane. The 4 lower sub-planes of the mental plane are referred to as the mental plane. Don't let this confuse you.

The causal body is the storehouse of lessons learned in an incarnation. Over the course of many lifetimes, virtuous qualities (selflessness, compassion, sympathy, humility, unconditional love) are developed in the causal body, enabling the Soul to express itself fully as resplendent Divine Light – the "Light of the Soul."

Ultimately, we are God in manifestation. One doesn't need to develop super psychic or spiritual powers to become a "god." The modern western mind reels at the idea man is God, but we share the same Consciousness as God.

The only thing that separates us from God is our egos/ personalities. Our job is to purify our egos/personalities so we can realize our own Divinity and Immortality. What are you waiting for?

We are immortal Souls

Forces Manifesting Through the Sun

When we think of light, we think of sunlight. Visible light is only a very small part of the electromagnetic radiation spectrum (a product of the nuclear fusion of hydrogen into helium) emanating from the sun.

Other types of electromagnetic radiation are infrared and ultraviolet rays, microwaves, radio and television waves, x-rays, and gamma rays, all of which are considered "light" by scientists. The electromagnetic radiation field not only gives us light, but heat, magnetism, electricity and chemical bonding – all basically the result of polarity.

Also emitted from the sun are alpha particles (helium) and beta particles (high-energy electrons). Cosmic rays are actually high-energy particles (not radiation/rays) emitted from astrophysical events occurring beyond our solar system. Cosmic background radiation, another phenomenon, is believed to be a result of the "Big Bang."

The purpose of this manual is sun gazing for spiritual transformation. We're not working directly with visible physical light or the electromagnetic spectrum, but rather with Light of a higher nature.* Ancient philosophers and mystics believed stars/suns were focal points for the manifestation of the physical universe from higher dimensions.

There are at least two higher dimensional forces manifesting through the sun (imbued within sunlight) – *Prana* and *Kundalini*. Fundamentally, *Prana* and *Kundalini* both emanate from the same source – the Solar *Logos*, although they perform different functions.

Some schools consider them to be entirely different forces while others believe they're the same thing. We'll describe *Prana* and *Kundalini* as two distinct forces while recognizing their ultimate essential oneness.

*To differentiate between Light of a higher nature and physical light, I'll capitalize the former and use the lower case l for the latter.

Prana

Prana is commonly believed to refer to human breath, but *Prana* is much, much more. Hindus call *Prana* the Breath of Life, the all-powerful, all-pervading rhythm of the universe. **_Prana_ is also the Creative Intelligent Life Force of the Universe.**

As Creative Intelligent Life Force, *Prana* is the direct link between matter and Spirit (God). Universal *Prana* permeates, informs, and sustains the Universe. **Consciousness and *Prana* (Cosmic Light)* are the basis of all matter and life.**

In a stricter sense, *Prana* is called Intelligent Life Force, or specific *Prana*. It organizes our individual cells into tissues and organs, and, eventually, forms the whole body and maintains the structure during our lifetimes. *Prana* also organizes and sustains our subtle bodies.

Through the etheric body as an interface medium, *Prana* informs/communicates between the subtle body and the physical body. *Prana* also informs the cells, fibers, nerves, and ganglia throughout the physical body. While *Prana* works primarily in the sympathetic, or involuntary system, it is involved in both sensory and motor activities.

Most importantly, for us, imbued within *Prana* are Divine Love and Wisdom. *Prana* not only vitalizes the physical and etheric bodies. It can purify the mental, emotional, and etheric bodies, thereby enabling the "Light of the Soul"** to shine forth. That's what spiritual transformation by sun gazing is all about.

*Prana is one example of Light of a higher nature.

**The "Light of the Soul" is another example.

Kundalini

Kundalini, or *Kundalini Shakti* (*Shakti* means Divine Will and Power), sometimes called the Serpent Power, is a type of *Prana*. Another name for it is *Prana Shakti*. *Kundalini* means "in a coil" (like a serpent), and this energy lies mostly dormant at the base of the spine in the root *chakra*. It's a latent creative force. While *Kundalini* is very important, we don't absorb it directly while sun gazing.

A force emanating from the Solar *Logos* ensouled the primordial "matter" making up the various planes and sub-planes of the Universe (not just the physical universe). *Kundalini* is this same force after it has reached its lowest immersion in matter and is ascending upwards through the planes back towards the Solar *Logos*. (From involution to evolution) Coming from deep within the earth, *Kundalini* is the force connecting man with the earth.

One of *Kundalini's* functions is to energize the etheric and subtle force centers (soon to be discussed). This primordial vital energy can be awakened and used for physical reproduction and rejuvenation **or** for spiritual evolvement. A small amount of *Kundalini* is already awake within us, involved with nerve flow and energizing the force centers at a minimum level necessary for life.

Most important for our work: *Kundalini* is directly related to our level of consciousness. When awakened properly, *Kundalini* in the root *chakra* will rise up the *Sushumna* (subtle spine) to the Crown center. Along the way, it brings consciousness to the higher centers. As you purify your subtle body, the *Kundalini* can rise rather than get trapped.

Warning: If *Kundalini* awakens prematurely, it will get trapped in the lower centers and intensify the physical experience. This occasionally happens when someone with the wrong motives incorrectly performs *Tantra* or other types of yoga that use sexual energy. One is drawn deeper into the physical world of sensory consciousness – not the direction you want to be going. We'll be getting into this further.

If a person doesn't have a high level of moral and ethical purity to control this powerful force, undesirable passions become impossible to control, turning him into a depraved monster. While one might gain certain supranormal intellectual and/or occult powers, these powers will be accompanied by selfishness, abnormal pride, and ruthless ambition.

Black magicians use *Kundalini* this way intentionally for power and control over others, but they eventually pay a terrible price, usually ending up broken and deranged, driven mad by their cruel, selfish actions.

Part III

Subtle Anatomy

"It must, however, be always clearly understood that, for our philosophers, spirit in this sense is subtle body, an embodiment of a finer order of nature than that known to physical sense and not soul proper. By body, moreover, is not meant developed and organized form, but rather 'essence' or 'plasm' that may be graded, or as it were woven into various textures. In itself unshaped, it is capable of receiving the impression or pattern of any organized form.

The Soul proper, on the contrary is thought of as utterly incorporeal. Psychic* (Soul) life is classified according to its manifestations in body, but is not itself body."

Doctrine of the Subtle Body in Western Tradition by G.R.S. Mead

Page 36

---

*To the ancient Greeks, *Psyche* was the personification of the Soul. In modern times, the word has an entirely different meaning.

Vehicles of the Soul

This book is about spiritual transformation. Spiritual transformation involves subtle psychology. Subtle psychology takes place in the realm of subtle anatomy. **Subtle anatomy is the mostly unseen part of man existing on other planes.** Subtle anatomy describes the causal body and subtle body, which are preexistent to your physical body and exist after your physical body perishes.

We don't have Souls. We are Souls. For a Soul to experience the lower planes/dimensions – causal, mental, astral and physical – it requires vehicles, or bodies. These bodies are made of "matter" of their respective planes/fields. The nature, or state, of each body conditions the Soul's experience <u>and</u> its expression. I use the words vehicles and bodies interchangeably.

The vehicles are: the **causal body**, the **mental body**, the **astral/emotional body**, the **etheric body*** – often referred to as the **Etheric Double,** and the **physical body**. Some schools consider the etheric body as part of the physical body, which, technically, it is (both are on the physical plane).

Some schools combine the etheric, astral/emotional, and mental bodies into one vehicle called the astral body. Others refer to some or all of these bodies as the subtle body. All of this can lead to confusion. I'll define my terms and try to be specific and consistent.

The human Soul (an individualized unit of Consciousness) resides in the <u>causal body</u> and enters the physical body in the medulla at conception. It's called the human Soul because it has to express itself through our personalities.

The causal body contains the blueprint (thoughts/ideas/*logoi*) for the various bodies, or vehicles, the Soul uses to function in the physical world (including the physical body). It's also the realm of intelligence, abstract thinking, and soul consciousness.

*I use the terms etheric body and Etheric Double interchangeably.

The causal body is made from the finest matter (highest vibrational rate) of the three higher sub-planes of the mental plane. It doesn't disintegrate after death like the astral and mental bodies eventually do.

The virtues we acquire from life to life are retained in the causal body as our spirits evolve. So is the karma accumulated from past incarnations needing to be worked out in this or future lifetimes. Eventually, we'll evolve to a state of consciousness where we won't need to incarnate on the physical plane. Or the astral, mental, or causal planes.

The mental body is composed of matter of the four lower sub-planes of the mental plane. The mental body is the vehicle through which the Soul manifests as concrete intellect (everyday tangible thinking) where the powers of the mind, including memory and imagination are developed.

It's your thought field – your mind. Technically, it's where your "mind" happens. The act of the Soul thinking sets the matter of the mental body into vibration. The resulting vibrating energy patterns are called thought-forms or, simply, thoughts.

The Soul uses the mind for perception of sense reality. The mind and the brain are not the same thing. The physical brain does not think. It's like a computer, registering and storing information. The brain also puts thoughts into action. It's the physical link between the mind and the sensory world (physical phenomena).

The shape of the mental body is ovoid and extends out about twice as far as the astral body, or about 3 feet, but most of the mental matter collects near the physical body.

The astral body, sometimes called the emotional body, is composed of denser (lower vibrational rate) matter than the mental body. The astral body is the vehicle in which feelings, passions, desires, and emotions are experienced and expressed. Feelings and emotions are specific vibrating energy patterns of astral matter similar to thought-forms.

The astral body acts as a bridge between the physical brain and the mind. It also makes sensation possible by translating information from the physical senses into sensations and then sending them to the mind (in the mental body) where they're perceived (perception). Therefore, I like to use the term "astral body" because this vehicle isn't only concerned with emotions. It's also the center of sensation.

The appearance of the astral body varies widely among people. In the average man, it extends about 18 inches beyond the physical body in an ovoid, or egg, shape (3D), though most of the astral matter gathers around the physical body. Depending on the intensity and quality of feelings (low or high-minded), the astral body displays a vivid colored pattern seen by the clairvoyant. But that's another story – an art and science unto itself.

In modern times, the astral and mental bodies are often collectively referred to as the <u>subtle body</u>. In order to explain spiritual psychology, it's sometimes easier if we distinguish between the astral/emotional and mental bodies. Other times, I'll refer to them collectively as the subtle body. Just remember, they're the <u>same</u> thing.

Remembering each plane has seven sub-planes, the physical body seen by most people is made of matter from the three lowest (most dense) sub-planes of the physical plane – solids, liquids and gases. The remaining four sub-planes make up what is referred to as the etheric plane (also considered part of the physical plane). <u>Every</u> solid, liquid, and gaseous particle of the physical body is interpenetrated with etheric matter.

The body composed of this matter is called the etheric body, or <u>Etheric Double</u>, and can be seen by those with clairvoyant abilities. It projects about a quarter of an inch beyond the skin. <u>The physical body is actually a denser exact duplicate of the etheric body.</u> The etheric body is, as are the other bodies, three-dimensional – not just a flat plane.

Not a vehicle of consciousness itself, the Etheric Double acts as an interface between the physical body and the astral body, transmitting impulses from the physical senses to the astral body and transmitting Consciousness from the higher planes to the brain and nervous system.

Informed by *Prana* (Creative Intelligent Life Force), the Etheric Double also translates information from the causal and subtle bodies to the electromagnetic field organizing the individual cells into the physical body. While DNA governs the production of cells, it doesn't direct them into tissues, organs, or a body. Remember: the Etheric Double emerges from the astral body and precedes the dense physical body.

Another important function of the Etheric Double is to transfer *Prana* from the Universal field to the individual field and thence to the physical body. It's the primary contact with the field of life energy (*Prana*, sometimes called Universal Life Energy) sustaining all of nature.

The Etheric Double also acts as a connecting link between the physical and subtle bodies. These bodies interpenetrate each other and are synchronized, thus constituting the vehicles of the Soul(conscious Self) during its incarnation in the physical world. Not as complicated as it sounds. The physical body and Etheric Double are inseparable in life, and the Etheric Double slowly disintegrates at the death of the physical body.

By means of the Etheric Double, we are conditioned and vitalized by the life force (*Prana*) which pours in through its major force centers, or *chakras* (soon to be discussed). At the same time, the force centers at the astral and mental levels are processing energy (*Prana*) from their fields, and this energy conditions and modifies the etheric energy as it flows through the network of channels in the Etheric Double called *Nadis*.

Luminous etheric channels of *Pranic* energy, or *Nadis,* also run parallel to the nervous system with which they interpenetrate and interface. (Probably, the luminous body referred to in some occult systems) That's how *Prana* interacts with the physical body.

The Etheric Double is the body most often depicted in pictures about subtle anatomy. You know the one. The pictures of a man with small colored circles on the midline of his head and torso.

It's this body we'll mostly be working with while sun gazing because *Prana* comes through the sun, and it works through the etheric body. Incoming *Prana* charges the etheric body and opens up the channels between the subtle body and the physical body. This is how the body is energized by sun gazing.

But wait! There's more. **Remember:** *Prana* is the Creative Intelligent Life Force of the Universe. Imbued within that force is Divine Love and Wisdom. *Prana* can purify the mental, astral, etheric and physical bodies. This leads to spiritual regeneration, or transformation. **Stay attuned!**

Diagram 1 (pg 77) offers a rough idea of how the subtle, etheric, and physical bodies relate to each other. Keep in mind, these bodies are really not layers as depicted for demonstration purposes. They fully inter-penetrate each other, being matter of different vibrational rates (like radio waves, television waves, ex-rays, and microwaves).

Also, remember they're all three-dimensional – not flat planes. The mental and astral bodies are ovoids, while the Etheric Double resembles the shape of the physical body. I couldn't find a simple drawing of the causal body. It's rarely observed.

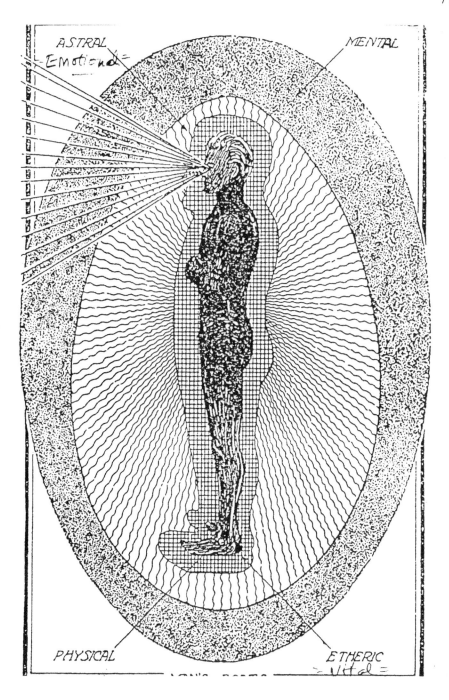

Diagram 1   The Subtle Body

The Aura

Ever wonder what the aura really is? It's not just a colorful psychic cloud hangin' around someone. It's the composite field of one's causal, mental, astral, and etheric bodies – the bodies extending beyond the dense physical body.

Although there are numerous descriptions of the aura, that's what it ultimately is. **The appearance of the aura depends greatly on the spiritual development of the observer as well as that of the subject.**

The astral layer shows man's passions, emotions, and feelings, depending on the mood of the person. The mental layer displays thought-forms which reveal the state of one's mind. The causal body is rarely developed enough to be seen in most people, but in someone advanced it's radiant in glorious light.

The "health aura" is actually the unused particles of *Prana* that are discharged from the body in all directions. Absorbing more than he needs, the healthy person radiates *Prana* from the Etheric Double outward which can strengthen and fortify those around him.

The Force Centers

The causal, mental, astral, and etheric bodies all have points of connection in which energy and information (vibrations) flow from one body to another. They're referred to as *chakras* (wheels), or force centers. I'll use the terms *chakra*, force center, and center interchangeably – for no particular reason.

<u>This exchange is one of the means by which the vehicles/bodies of the Soul communicate with each other and how the Soul interacts with the physical body.</u> **The force centers are also considered as centers of Consciousness.**

The force centers are both transmitters and transformers of energy/information between the causal, mental, astral, and etheric bodies. They slow down or speed up the vibrational rate of the energy from each field, or plane, so the bodies can interact. I know that sounds pretty vague, but it's the best description I've been able to find.

The causal field is of a higher vibrational rate than the mental field, which is of a higher vibrational rate than the astral field, which is of a higher vibrational rate than the etheric field. The force centers synchronize the flow of the causal, mental, astral, and etheric energies.

The force centers depicted in numerous references are the Etheric Double centers, which can be seen by many clairvoyants. They look like rapidly spinning vortices which draw in energy towards their centers in a tight flow and radiate it outward to the periphery of the force centers in ever widening spirals.

I don't have the ability to see *chakras*, so I can only go by what I read as to what they look like. Most often, they're portrayed as colored discs, one for every color of the rainbow,* although I don't know if anybody really sees them in this way. Sometimes, complex symbols are overlaid on drawings of the force centers. These are used as teaching aids – not meant to be representative of what the *chakras* look like.

*Some schools use different color schemes. Not too important.

In some works, the *chakras* described by clairvoyants are much more complex looking and multicolored. I think this is probably the most accurate. Remember: the force centers consist of different frequencies of *Prana*. They're reported to vary greatly from one person to the next. It doesn't really matter what they look like. We're concerned with what they do.

Keep in mind, these force centers aren't actually structures but are vortices, or whirlpools, of <u>energy *(Prana)*</u>. The force centers appear as saucer-like depressions on the surface of the etheric body. Looking straight on, the center appears as the bell of a flower. From a side view, the stalk of the flower comes from a point in the spine leading to the bell-shaped vortice on the anterior surface of the etheric body.

Their size and appearance vary greatly depending on the level of their development and activity. In an undeveloped person, they appear small and sluggish, just barely functioning. In someone more evolved, they are brilliantly glowing and pulsating with living light.

There are at least several different *chakra*, or force center, schools of thought. Usually, the centers are organized along the cerebrospinal axis. Most of the centers are related to various nerve plexuses emanating from the spinal cord. Others are related to areas of the brain. Sometimes, they're associated with various endocrine glands and organs.

Here are the major differences I've found between various systems:

The subtle stalk of the solar plexus center follows the spinal nerves radiating from the midthoracic spine near the level of the anatomical solar plexus – the area just below the sternum. These nerves travel down and outward to the umbilical region on the anterior of the body where the force center is located. So, the actual solar plexus center is not anywhere near the anatomical solar plexus. This can cause confusion.

The solar plexus center actually gets its name because of the twelve large nerve ganglia radiating like rays of the sun from that area. It's also called, variously, the umbilical, navel, or lumbar center because of its location. I'll refer to it as the solar plexus center.

Another issue is the sacral center, which isn't referred to by some schools. These schools are aware of the danger of this force center being awakened and avoid working with it. Other systems include it. I'll mention it only to point out its negative effect on spiritual evolvement.

Activating this force center will only pull one down deeper into sense-mind consciousness. Black magicians use the lower force centers to energize their bad behavior – seeking power or control over others. This is utilizing *Prana* and *Kundalini* in the wrong way.

Some schools teach about the splenic center, which absorbs *Prana* for vitality and distributes it throughout the body. The center is located off to the left of the midline, near the spleen. Other schools consider the activities of this center to take place in the sacral center and don't mention the splenic center as a distinct *chakra*.

Some references don't include the Crown and/or brow *chakras* as part of their system. They're regarded as centers of higher consciousness. So, sometimes you end up with five or six *chakras* in the system.

I put together a working *chakra* system based on several schools of thought (Eastern and Western). For the most part, it's the standard *chakra* system. I just threw in the splenic *chakra* to make it complete even though it's not a center of Consciousness.

Chakras

Crown/Coronal/*Sahasrara**   on the top of the head

Brow/"Spiritual Eye"/*Anja*   in the forehead area between
the eyebrows

Throat/Cervical/*Vishudda*   at the front of the throat

Heart/Dorsal/*Anahata*   over the heart

Splenic/*Surya*   left of the centerline in the
area of the spleen

Solar Plexus/Navel/Lumbar/*Manipura* in the area of the navel

Sacral/*Svadhisthana*   in the sacral region

Root/Coccygeal/ *Muladhara*   at the base of the spine

See **Diagram 2** pg 87

* *Sanskrit* system

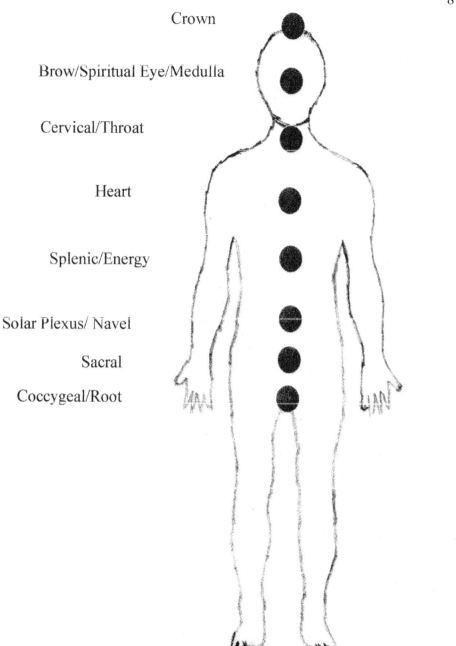

Crown

Brow/Spiritual Eye/Medulla

Cervical/Throat

Heart

Splenic/Energy

Solar Plexus/ Navel

Sacral

Coccygeal/Root

CHAKRA/FORCE CENTER SYSTEM

Diagram 2

I guess it's as good as any, and it works for what we need to do. If you don't like it, use your own. I'm hoping people won't get too hung up if it varies from the system they've learned. I don't think peoples or cultures have different force centers – just different ways of talking about them.

Please excuse the casual attitude. It's just not really that important for what we're trying to do. Few people can see them, and I think the *chakra* system offered will be good enough for our purposes. Fortunately, *Kundalini* and *Prana* will do the work for us. Mostly, we'll be concentrating on the Crown *chakra*, the "Spiritual Eye," and the heart center.

The following is a general description of the centers. I'll get into specifics later when necessary. Note: there are numerous centers of force and energy in the body. We're concentrating on the major force centers related to the cerebrospinal system (brain and spinal cord) and considered to be centers of Consciousness.

The coccygeal center, or root *chakra*, at the base of the spine, is where *Kundalini* wells up in the body from the center of the earth. This primordial vital energy can serve either the functions of physical reproduction and rejuvenation (when the energy is directed to the sacral center) or be used for spiritual enlightenment (when the energy is directed to the Crown center).

The sacral center is the realm of sexual energy and the repro-ductive force. In some schools, this center is said to also be involved with *Prana*.

Although we are not here concerned with the splenic center (it's not directly involved with spiritual psychology or transformation), it does play an important role in sustaining the etheric body by absorbing *Prana* and distributing it to the other centers to maintain life.

The splenic center, or *Surya* (sun) chakra, **isn't** considered a center of Consciousness. Some schools consider it an independent force center left of the midline just below the ribs. Other schools believe its functions take place in area of the sacral center.

The solar plexus center gets its name from the dense concentration of nerve fibers "radiating" from it resembling rays of the sun. The solar plexus (also called the lumbar, navel, or umbilical center) is associated with feelings and emotions and is thus very involved in the emotional life. In most people, the solar plexus is the most important and active of all centers.

This center is active in persons with strong desires and plays an important role in projection of personal energy (spontaneously or intentionally). It's believed to be linked with the liver and the stomach. The central and sympathetic nervous systems link together in the solar plexus. The solar plexus is a focal point in spiritual transformation, which is our main concern.

The heart center reflects the quality and power of unconditional love in one's life. When a person has transformed personal desires and passions into a wider and more universal compassion and love for others, the heart center becomes the focus of energies which were formally concentrated in the solar plexus. **Very Important!**

The heart center has a close relationship with the Crown center. Focusing on the heart center during meditation can strengthen the connection with the core of the Crown center. The heart center is the point of integration for the whole *chakra* system and is a primary factor in spiritual transformation. **The Soul expresses itself through this center.**

The throat center is associated with vibration. It's involved with sensitivity to color and form as well as sound and rhythm. The throat center links with the Crown center and the "Spiritual Eye" in certain states of expanded consciousness. When awakened, it's the center of clair-audience.

The medulla (part of the brain stem) is where the Soul enters the physical body. It's the "seat of life." Remember, consciousness and life are from the subtle body. On the physical level, nerves originating from the medulla innervate the heart and diaphragm by way of the vagus nerve, regulating the heartbeat and breathing – both which are essential for life.

On the subtle level, it's called the "mouth of God" and is connected with the "Spiritual Eye." The subtle medulla and the "Spiritual Eye" can be regarded together as one force center for our work. One source says the "Spiritual Eye" is the subtle medulla. We'll consider them as a working unit. Perhaps, the subtle medulla can be thought of as the subtle brain stem center and the "Spiritual Eye" as the bell-like flower of the *chakra*.

Most schools don't consider the medulla as a center of Consciousness, but one highly regarded school goes into great detail about its importance in the elevation and expansion of consciousness. (See The "Spiritual Eye" (pg 127)

The "Spiritual Eye", or brow center, while not part of the physical brain, is located in the area of the frontal part of the brain between the eyebrows. Sometimes it's referred to as the "third eye."

It's the organ of visualization and the center of perception which may be directed outwardly to the external world, or inwardly to the realm of Spirit. The "Spiritual Eye" is associated with the pituitary gland, which regulates hormonal production. (Some report it's associated with the pineal gland)

The Crown center, or thousand petal lotus (KPL), at the top of the cerebrum, is the seat of the Soul. It can be referred to as the subtle brain. The Crown center is the realm of higher consciousness and is dormant in most people. It's associated with the pineal gland.

The internal consciousness of most people operates only from the three lowest centers – solar plexus, sacral, and coccygeal – the realm of the sense mind. For our purposes, we are concerned with elevating our consciousnesses to the higher centers.

The heart center is the gateway to the centers of higher consciousness – cervical/throat, medulla/brow/"Spiritual Eye," and Crown *chakras*. That's why we'll stress the heart center in our work. Now, it's time to see how the vehicles of the Soul and the force centers are related to consciousness.

Part IV

Subtle Psychology

"Subtle psychology, a relatively new term, describes the interactions between the Soul and the spirit. These interactions are the foundation of spiritual transformation. Subtle psychology explains what's actually going on during spiritual transformation. Many terms need to be defined."

author

Soul and Spirit Defined

The terms "Spirit" and "Soul" are not always clearly defined. Often, they're used interchangeably which can lead to confusion and misunderstanding. I'll define them for our purposes.

First, there is Absolute Spirit. This is God – indescribable, ineffable, beyond eternal, and infinite. Omnipotent. Omniscient. Omnipresent. Absolute Spirit willed Creation into being. Absolute Spirit/God can also be referred to as Consciousness.

Consciousness manifests as Divine Light. The Soul is an individualized ray of that Divine Light. We <u>are</u> Souls. How can anyone deny our Divine Nature? The ancient Greek philosophers and *Gnostic* mystics referred to the Soul as the "light spark" or "light seeds." (Some can see these "sparks" emanating from the heart center of a spiritually awakened person.) **The Soul is immortal.**

The Soul is an individualized unit of Consciousness. For our purposes, the pure Soul is the Consciousness within us that makes us conscious of our feelings, will, cognition (sensation, perception, conception) and our environment.

The Soul is the "Witness" that's aware of what's going on. The Soul uses the mind and body to interact with physical reality. That's how God experiences Creation– through our Souls. The Soul can also be considered as the higher Self, "the Christ within," and the "*Buddha* nature."

The human Soul (residing in the causal body) enters the physical body in the medulla at physical conception. As already mentioned, the causal body contains the blue-print (thoughts/ideas/*logoi*) for the various bodies, or vehicles, the Soul uses to function in the physical world.

The developed causal body has been referred to as the *Augoeides*, which means luminous, or radiant, body. In *The Untitled Apocalypse* (renamed *The Gnosis of the Light*) from the *Codex Brucianus* – a Coptic *Gnostic* treatise, the *Augoeides* is called the "Starry Body."

Superimposed and interpenetrating the causal body are the mental and emotional/astral bodies. Although the Soul is not confined by these bodies, for visualization purposes it helps to think of It as the core surrounded by the mental and astral bodies.

The mental and astral bodies together are often called the subtle body. The bodies of the subtle body interact with and influence each other as well as the causal, etheric, and the dense physical bodies. The subtle body conditions the experience and expression of the Soul.

The Neoplatonists referred to the subtle body of the Soul as the "spirituous," or "spirit," body. Not to be confused with Absolute Spirit or the "Holy Spirit/Ghost" – something else entirely. **They described the spirit as an embodiment of a finer order of matter than the physical body, but not as the Soul itself.**

This body is not developed and organized but rather a "plasm" of different grades woven into various textures. This is exactly how the mental and astral bodies have been described. **So, it's correct to refer to the subtle body as the spirit. Think of the spirit as the subtle embodiment of the Soul.** Or think of the spirit as a lens through which the "Light of the Soul" shines forth.

In Greek mythology, *Psyche* (a goddess) is the personification of the Soul. Over time, *psyche* has come to mean the human faculty for thought, judgment, and emotion. It's the totality of the human mind – conscious and subconscious. That describes the subtle body (astral/emotional and mental bodies). **So, the *psyche* can be equated with the subtle body and the spirit.**

In the ancient Greek theater, actors wore masks to conceal their true identities and become someone else – their character, or ***persona***. That's exactly what the Soul does when it expresses itself through the mental body (thoughts) and the astral body (emotions and feelings) *i.e.* your subtle body.

The Soul takes on the "personality" (mask) of the subtle body. To go one step further, the personality can be considered as one's "spirit," or "nature." "Mean-spirited" or "good-natured." When you look at it this way, a lot of things can be tied together.

Some Greek philosophers described it another way. They believed there were two kinds of Souls: the rational soul and the irrational soul. The rational soul was considered to be the pure Soul, a ray of the *Logos*. The *Logos* represented ratio, harmony, and reason. The rational soul is one's Higher Self, or true spiritual nature.

The irrational soul, a distorted reflection of the rational soul, is out of harmony with the *Logos* and without Divine reason. It's one's lower self, or pseudo-soul – the animal nature.

They suggested most men have a mixture of these two parts. Thus, Souls were referred to as composite, with the rational and irrational souls struggling for dominance. **Of course, we really have only one Soul. In fact, we ultimately all share the <u>same</u> Soul. What differentiates us is our spirits/personalities/egos.**

The *Essene* "Doctrine of the Two Spirits" states man has a light spirit, or nature, <u>and</u> a dark spirit, or nature. While it seems this can actually be observed by some, we really only have one spirit that can be pure (light), or impure (dark), to a varying amount of degree. The same spirit can go either way. It's the purity of the spirit that determines how much the "Light of the Soul" shines through and whether the spirit appears "light" or "dark."

The *Pythagoreans*, the *Essenes*, and the *Theraputae* were all described as "physicians of the Soul." Technically, they were physicians of the spirit/subtle body. **The Soul is already perfect and immortal. The Soul is an individualized ray of Divine Light – the Consciousness of God.**

How can the Soul get any better than that without merging entirely back into Absolute Spirit beyond Vibratory Creation? It's the Soul's vehicles that need to be healed/purified. And that's what we're workin' on.

The ancient Greek philosophers and *Gnostics* lamented and bemoaned the sufferings of the Soul in this world. They considered it to be a prison, even a tomb, for the Soul. But, in reality, it's the thoughts and emotions of the ego/subtle body that make the Soul suffer in this world. They're the prison.*

Fortunately, thoughts and emotions can be changed or controlled. When the ego is subdued and one lives in soul consciousness and higher states, the Kingdom of God (the *Pleroma*) can be experienced on earth, at least for that person. That's our goal.

As previously mentioned, the Soul is already perfect – made in the Image of God. The spirit limits the expression of the Soul. This book is about **spirit--ual** transformation. **Spiritual transformation, or regeneration, takes place in the subtle body/spirit.**

In order to experience spiritual transformation, at least in a positive manner, one must purify one's thoughts (mental body) and emotions/ feelings (astral body) *i.e* the subtle body/spirit. When the spirit is purified, the "Light of the Soul" shines through. Put another way, you're "born again in spirit."

This was the goal of the various Ancient Mystery Schools, the *Hermetic Gnostics*, *Mithraists*, early alchemists, pre-Christian *Gnostics*, early Jewish and Christian mystics, and many other schools. There are many ways of looking at the same thing. There's **only** One God/Absolute Spirit/ Consciousness.

*The physical plane is where we (as Souls) **need** to be to purify our subtle bodies and work out our *karma*. It's all part of the evolutionary process.

Ego

Ego is the Latin word for "**I**." To many, ego has a variety of meanings: self-esteem, inflated sense of self-worth, the conscious thinking self, and **a sense of individual identity**. The ego is not an organ or a group of brain cells. It's not a physical structure. It's not a neurochemical event. **Ego <u>happens/is</u> in the subtle body (mental and astral bodies).**

For our purposes, the Soul is an individualized unit of Consciousness – our true nature. **<u>The ego is the Soul expressing itself through the subtle body/spirit.</u>** So, although I often refer to the Soul and the ego as two different entities, they're actually the same thing – just from different perspectives.*

When the ego/personality is pure – free of hangups, delusions, prejudices, and misconceptions – the Soul can express itself properly through the ego and interact with the physical world <u>and</u> the spiritual world. Then we are in a state of <u>soul</u> <u>consciousness</u>. But when the ego is impure, it distorts the expression of the Soul, resulting in body-identified <u>ego</u> <u>consciousnesses</u>. The ego thinks <u>it's</u> all you are.

Opinions, beliefs, likes, dislikes, reactions, and perceptions are all part of our past programming and conditioning. They cloud/filter/limit the Soul's experience and expression. When they're deeply ingrained in our psyches/spirits, they're called *samskaras* by the Eastern Teachers. There are both positive and negative *samskaras*. In fact, the sum total of all *samskaras* **is** the ego. This all takes place in the subtle body (astral/emotional and mental bodies).

When distorted or impure, the ego becomes a shroud which veils our essential oneness with God and each other. Ego is driven by material desires, emotions, habits, and undisciplined sense inclinations. The faults of the ego are: lust/desire, anger, arrogance, greed, delusion, pride, envy, and material attachment.

*Some schools refer to the pure <u>Ego</u> <u>as</u> the Soul – the Image of God in man. They distinguish between the pure <u>Ego</u> (higher Self/Soul) and its reflection – the <u>ego</u> (lower self/pseudo-soul/counterfeit spirit).

*(continued) Higher Self and lower self are just other ways to respectively describe the Soul and the ego. The Self can mean anything from the Solar *Logos*/Spiritual Sun, to the *Monad*, to the Individualized Soul, depending on which plane it's working through. The lower self is the pseudo-soul, or ego.

Thoughts, Feelings, and *Samskaras*

Now that we've defined the Soul, spirit, and ego and introduced the struggle going on between the Soul and the ego for our identity, let's explain how *samskaras* are created.

Remember: man – a Soul – is individualized Consciousness. When the Soul thinks a thought, a vibration is created in the matter of the mental body. From there, the vibration goes through the astral and etheric bodies before it triggers the neurons in the physical brain.

Every definite thought produces two effects – a radiating vibration and a floating form of <u>mental</u> matter. When someone directs a thought towards external objects of desire or is occupied with emotional activities, a radiating vibration and a floating form are produced in the <u>astral</u> body.

Most thoughts are influenced by desire, passion, or emotion. So, the resulting thought-emotion form (vibrating energy pattern) is made up of both mental and astral matter and remains in the mental and astral bodies unless a strong emotion projects it outwards (intentionally or unintentionally), at least temporarily. Eventually, it will return to its originator. In other words, your thought-emotion forms hang around you.

The longevity of a thought-emotion form depends on its initial intensity and its repetition. The more often it's repeated, the firmer it become entrenched in the matter of the subtle body. These forms react on the person who created them and regenerate themselves.*

*The radiating vibration will also duplicate its own frequency on any mental body it contacts, reproducing the original thought in the other's mental body. The effect is dependent on the clearness, strength, and focus of the thought. This is how negative mental influence (black magic) works – psychically harming someone, or programming or manipulating them. But that's another story. The practice of such psychic chicanery not only harms your fellows. It's also very <u>self</u> limiting/<u>self</u>-destructive.

Long brooding and wallowing can create thought-emotion forms of tremendous power lasting for years, even lifetimes. Remember: these thought-emotion forms determine how you think, feel, look at the world, and experience life. **They precondition your subconscious mind and cause you to think and respond in a certain manner.**

Most people live in a prison of their own making, surrounded by masses of forms created by their thoughts and feelings. This is great when you have positive thoughts and emotions, but when your thoughts and emotions are negative, you're establishing prejudiced and fixed moods or attitudes that will prevent you from elevating and expanding your consciousness.

To make matters worse, because these thought-emotion forms are in your subtle body, they can stick with you from incarnation to incarnation. In fact, that's what reincarnation is all about – freeing your subtle body from habitual negative thoughts, attitudes, and tendencies so you can be conscious on the higher planes. Something you have to do during incarnation on the physical plane.

The *Sanskrit* word for one of these habitual thought-emotion forms (vibrating energy patterns) is a *samskara*. *Samskaras* can be prenatal – carried over from past lives, or postnatal – created by thoughts and actions during one's current incarnation. There are both positive and negative *samskaras*.

We'll be talking mostly about negative *samskaras* lurking in the subconscious mind that rob us of our free will and the discriminative power of the conscious mind. *Samskaras* are preprogrammed thoughts, feelings, and responses towards others, events, and situations.

Compulsions, identifications, attachments, aversions, addictions, and ambitions are types of negative *samskaras*. **<u>Purification of the subtle body breaks us free of our *samskaras*.</u>**

Soul Consciousness vs
Ego Consciousness

Now, it's time to discuss the apparent struggle between the Soul and the ego.

Soul consciousness is sometimes called super consciousness because, when you're in soul consciousness, you're guided by the higher faculties (intelligence, wisdom, and intuition) of the Soul rather than the conscious and subconscious minds which rely only on information from the senses. The conscious mind is what you're aware of at the moment. The subconscious mind is everything else in your mind.

Soul consciousness can also be called causal consciousness because the human Soul resides in the causal body on the causal plane. Soul consciousness is the beginning of being "in the Self."

When you're in a state of soul consciousness or higher states, you realize you're more than just your body. In fact, **you realize you're not your body at all.** You can feel it. When you look out your eyes, you get a sense you're really not part of your body. You're just usin' it like a space suit to experience the lower planes.

You also understand you're not your personality. Thoughts and emotions pop up into your awareness, but you don't identify with them. You can look at your so <u>very</u> important <u>s</u>elf and chuckle: "What a moron." Makes life a lot easier. You get to blame it on someone else. (Humor)

You <u>know</u> you're an immortal Soul – a ray of God's Divine Light. You **realize** you're of the same essence as God. By definition, this is *Gnosis*, or Self-Realization. You're aware of your essential unity with God and every other living being.

You realize this because you can feel it. You feel the unity, the Love, and the Bliss. You feel unconditional love, compassion, tolerance, sympathy, and understanding towards your fellows. They are just other versions of "you."

What is ego consciousness? First, we must remember the ego **is** the Soul working through the personality in the astral and mental bodies. Therefore, the Soul is influenced by the thoughts, opinions, likes and dislikes, emotions, and feelings in our astral and mental bodies.

Recap: The ego is our thoughts, opinions, likes and dislikes, emotions, and feelings. The personality is also our thoughts, opinions, likes and dislikes, emotions, and feelings. That's how we're able to equate personality with ego.

Sense-mind consciousness is the Soul as the ego working through the mind and the senses. When the Soul, working through the mind, is solely occupied with the senses and the physical world and not aware of It's spiritual reality, the result is the **sense-bound mind.**

Ego consciousness is when you identify only with your personality and your mind-body, rather than with your divine nature as an immortal Soul, a ray of Divine Light. That's why the ego is called the pseudo-soul. When one is established in ego consciousness, he's a **counterfeit soul**. The ego becomes an impostor, robbing you of your true identity.

Ego consciousness causes us to believe ourselves separate from everyone else and God and forgetful of our own true spiritual nature. This forgetfulness is depicted in an allegory of Plato – drinking from the river of *Lethe*/forgetfulness, the *Gnostic* poem *Hymn of the Pearl*, the *Bhagavad-Gita/Song of the Spirit*, the story of *Narcissus*, and *The Iliad and the Odyssey*, to name but a few.

The body identified ego, sense-bound mind, and ego conscious- ness are basically the same state of contracted consciousness. How does one rise above ego consciousness?

By purifying the spirit/subtle body with Divine Light manifesting as *Prana* which is imbued with Love and Wisdom, thereby freeing the spirit from the grip of *samskaras*. But first, we need to explain how one gets into a state of sense-bound mind.

Perception

How does the Soul become totally identified with the sense-bound mind rather than Its true spiritual nature? To understand that, we need to know how the Soul experiences the physical world.

Consciousness, <u>as</u> the Soul (a ray of Divine Light), resides in the causal Crown chakra and enters the physical body through the subtle* medulla (in the Etheric Double) by way of the causal spine known as the *brahmanadi*. The *brahmanadi* is pure Consciousness, not a structure.

From there, Consciousness, <u>as</u> the *brahmanadi,* expands outward and enters the three <u>subtle</u> spines – the inner *Chitra* (which controls activities related to consciousness), the middle *Vajra* (which controls activities of the subtle body), and the outer <u>subtle</u> *Sushumna.*

The *Sushumna* interpenetrates and interfaces with the nerves, spinal cord and brain of the central nervous system. On one side of the subtle *Sushumna* is the subtle *Ida* and on the other side is the subtle *Pingala,* both which interpenetrate and interface with the physical sympathetic ganglionic chains, one chain on each side running parallel to the spinal cord. They are the three largest channels of subtle energy and are called *Nadis.*

Consciousness is conveyed by the *Ida*, *Pingala*, and *Sushumna* which communicate with the sympathetic ganglionic chains and the brain, spinal cord, and nerves of the central nervous system by means of *Prana.* A minimum amount of *Kundalini* is also involved.

This is how Consciousness (Soul) experiences the etheric body and the dense physical body. The Etheric Double is an exact duplicate of the physical visible body, particle for particle, and is the medium for all the electrical and vital currents of the body.

*For our purposes, subtle refers to anything beyond the three lowest sub-levels of the physical plane – solids, liquids, and gases. We'll refer to the Etheric Double as subtle even though technically it's in the upper four sub-planes of the physical plane because few can see it.

The central and sympathetic nervous systems are informed/stimulated by the sense receptors (eyes, ears, nose, touch, taste, temp, pain, pressure). The sense receptors <u>only receive information</u> from the external world and convert it into electrical nerve impulses. The sense receptors don't **feel** anything.

Prana is the controlling energy which acts throughout the nerve-centers. The *Prana* coursing along nerves is distinct and separate from the electrical nerve impulses which are generated within the body.* *Prana* in the Etheric Double runs along the nerves of the body and enables them to act as carriers of external information from the senses.

The nerve impulses from the sense receptors are transmitted through the etheric body by *Prana* to the sense centers (not the major force centers) in the **kamic** sheath (center of sensation) of the astral body. The sense centers are where sharp, acute, and specific sensations are perceived.

Sensations begin as vibrations of our own nervous system. The nervous system is the contact between the physical and subtle worlds. Our physical nerves become subtler and subtler until they are actually vibrations in the Etheric Double and the subtle body.

So, impressions from the physical universe impinge on the material molecules of the dense physical body setting in vibration the cells of the organs of sensations, or our "senses." These vibrations in turn set in motion the finer molecules of the corresponding sense organs in the Etheric Double. Then, these vibrations pass to the astral body and the kamic sheath where sensations are experienced.

*The electrical nerve impulses work their way back up the nervous system to the brain where they trigger the proper neurological response, but this is not what gives us "feelings," or sensations.

"Feelings" can refer to both sensations or emotions. We're talking about sensations here.

From there, these vibrations initiate a response in the mental body where **perception** occurs. Then, they're reflected back through the astral body and Etheric Double, before finally reaching the neurons of the cerebral hemispheres. This gives us "normal brain consciousness," or the **sense mind.**

The brain merely receives vibrations. The astral body changes the vibrations into sensations, and the mental body changes the sensations into perceptions. The mind is the Soul expressing itself in the mental body. Most of us do not separate our-Selves from our mind-bodies. We think this is all we are.

We must learn to separate our Self (Soul) from our body, step out of it, and know we exist in a far fuller consciousness outside of it then within it. Once we realize this, any further identification of our Self with our bodies is impossible. This gives us a new perspective on "death." What we call "death" is really just **life** on another plane.*

Time for a little recap. What comes to our physical senses is energy in the form of vibrations of different frequencies. We think what we "perceive" in our minds is actually going on outside ourselves, beyond the senses. We experience the world as a series of sensory phenomena.

What actually comes to our senses are vibrating energy patterns of different frequencies. Our sense receptors are triggered by these vibrations and send nerve impulses which are carried by *Prana* to the astral body. Then to the mental body, where a picture is created in our mind of what exists. So, our astral and mental bodies not only condition our experience. They help create it.

This is how the Soul experiences the body and the outside world. This is how it's supposed to work. The problem arises when the Soul loses awareness of its true divine nature and becomes identified **solely** with the body and its experiences as Itself. This can be called body-identified consciousness, sense-bound mind consciousness, and/or ego conscious-ness– all basically the same state of contracted consciousness.

*Remember: The Soul is immortal.

Sense-Bound Mind

What is the sense-bound mind and what causes the mind to be sense bound? Time to explain.

The causal body is the realm of abstract thinking, but, more importantly, it's the home of the human Soul with its *buddhi* intelligence, discriminative wisdom, and intuition. The causal body is in the three upper sub-planes of the mental plane. Consciousness (as the Soul)* in the causal body is sometimes referred to as Upper *Manas*. In *Sanskrit, Manas* means "the thinker."

The mental body is in the four lower sub-planes of the mental plane. It's where concrete thinking, imagination, memory, and all other mental functions happen. Consciousness in the mental body is referred to as Lower *Manas*. For all practical purposes, Lower *Manas* can be called the "mind."

Remember the *kamic* sheath in the astral body – the center of sensation? The place where we experience the vibrations from our senses? Through our nervous systems, these vibrations are carried by *Prana* to the *kamic* sheath. *Kama* is the principle of sensation that translates physical vibrations into feeling in the astral body.

Kama, dwelling in the coccygeal center, has been described as the life principle of the astral body. *Kama* gives us feeling – both physical sensation and emotion. *Kama* includes feelings of every kind.

Physical needs (hunger, thirst, sexual desire), passions (lower forms of love, hatred, envy, and jealousy), pleasure and pain, and a desire for experiencing the physical world are the result of *Kama*. *Kama* pulls us away from soul consciousness towards sense-mind consciousness. It's the force that compels us to expand outward into the physical world.

*Remember: The Soul **is** an individual unit of Consciousness.

Kama is also the force of desire. Desire is moved to activity by attractions or repulsions from surrounding objects according to whether they give pleasure (not pain) or pain. *Kama* is the desire to indulge in sensory temptations and seek satisfaction and pleasure.

Driven by *Kama*, the ego strives to satisfy its insatiable desires. *Kama* causes us to express our basest instincts. It seeks gratification, wealth, status, power, domination – all things satisfying the sense-bound egotistical man.

Kama Manas (Desire-Mind), the union of *Kama* with Lower *Manas*, gives us **sense-bound mind** – our normal brain intelligence (normal conscious awareness). It's the rational* physical intellect of man bound by the senses. The sense-bound mind creates material desire and **attachment**.

Kama Manas is the sense-bound lower self (pseudo-soul, or ego) which imagines itself to be our true identity. *Kama Manas* is a part of the human personality and it functions in and through the physical brain. You could call *Kama Manas* a state of mind – a perspective or level of consciousness. So, ***Kama Manas* is the sense bound-mind which causes ego consciousness.**

There's nothing inherently wrong with the sense mind. You need it to function in physical "reality" – the 3-D space time continuum. You just don't want to be controlled by it. You want the Soul to be in charge, manifesting as soul consciousness with its faculties of *buddhi* intelligence, discriminative wisdom, and intuition rather than be driven by the whims and cravings of *Kama Manas* – the sense-bound mind.

*Here, rational refers to to the sense-bound intellect without the intuitive intelligence of the Soul.

Kama, Lower *Manas*, and Upper *Manas*

How do we get out of sense-bound mind/ego consciousness? One thing we need to do is disentangle Lower *Manas* from *Kama*. Consider Lower *Manas* (the mind) to be a battlefield where the higher Self/Soul and the lower self/ego struggle for control.

Free will resides in Upper *Manas*. <u>It's by our thoughts that desires can be changed and controlled.</u> Thought awareness and thought control. Desire towards outward objects must become Will which seeks soul consciousness within. **It's up to us.**

The discriminative wisdom tendencies of the Soul's pure intelligence (*buddhi**) of Upper *Manas* (in the causal body) can overcome the tendencies of the sense-bound mind (*Kama Manas*). <u>Lower *Manas* (your mind) must identify with the *buddhi* intelligence of Upper *Manas* in the causal body instead of *Kama* in the astral body.</u>

To break free from *Kama*, Lower *Manas* must <u>unite</u> with Upper *Manas*. Then, you can move away from Desire and outward expression into the physical universe towards Will and inward to <u>Spirit</u> – pulled by *buddhi* intelligence, discriminative wisdom, and intuition. By freeing yourself from *Kama* and ego consciousness, you can **realize**** soul consciousness.

*Buddhi means to be awake, to know, to understand, to be conscious again. It's the faculty of intuitive discernment, or direct spiritual awareness. *Buddhi* intelligence is the wisdom of the Soul.

**For our purposes, <u>realize</u> means to experience something.

On the lower planes, the Soul has to work through the medium of the personal self, or personality. The Souls of all men are of the same essence and substance. The difference between a spiritual man and a cruel, selfish, tyrant is the quality and makeup of the subtle body (personality) through which the Soul manifests. That's why we need to purify our personalities/spirits/subtle bodies.

To repeat: Lower *Manas* (in the mental body) must breakaway from *Kama* (in the astral body) and link with Upper *Manas* (in the causal body). Then, the lower self is under control of the higher Self.* The personality is now guided by the Soul instead of the ego. This is the "mystical marriage" of some esoteric traditions.

In the Eastern teachings, the link between the lower self and the higher Self is called the *antahkarana* – sometimes referred to as the "Bridge of Light." By strengthening the link between the Soul and the personality, they will gradually come to function as one entity, with the Soul in control (soul consciousness). **This is done by purifying the personality/spirit so the mind and the brain can respond to the vibrations of the Soul.**

We'll be telling your how to do this. In fact, I've already given you the techniques for that, so you're probably already on your Way! Fortunately, performing the techniques is a lot easier than explainin' what's going on. Of course, there's a little more to it. (Hint – **detachment**) In the next few chapters, I'll elaborate.

*Remember: For our work, the ego is the lower self. The Soul is the higher Self.

Intellect, Intelligence, and Intuition
Elevation and Expansion
Inward and Outward

This is a little side chapter to define a few terms and explain some concepts.

Intellect* – the rational mind– is Lower *Manas*. Intellect is knowledge, facts, and information. It can be developed by education and study. We use intellect to "reason." Reason is a process of passing through a series of judgments in order to reach a conclusion.

Unfortunately, reason is guided by the imperfect intellect, which is influenced by opinions, emotions, desires, and habits and is dependent on the senses. Even the best intellectual reasoning is prone to error.

Intelligence is the wisdom of the Soul. Intelligence evaluates how to use knowledge, facts, and information wisely. To see the "big picture." Wisdom guides the intellect into making the right decision. Wisdom comes from the *buddhi* intelligence of Upper *Manas*. **

Discriminative wisdom flows from intuition and is obtained through contact with the Soul – soul consciousness. Discrimination born of intuition ensures right judgment in any given situation. The Soul, through intuition, offers intuitive guidance manifesting as wisdom to guide intellect, or reason, to the right determination. Wisdom from *buddhi* intelligence is "pure reason." This intuition will guide your spiritual evolution.

*To the Neoplatonists, intellect meant *nous* – the higher faculties of the mind *i.e.* Upper *Manas*. It can get a bit tricky trying to cross reference different schools of thought, particularly when they span thousands of years.

** The higher the plane, the higher the level of consciousness.

True intuition comes from the Soul. It's the voice of your higher Self guiding you. Leading you to making the correct decision in any situation. If there's the least bit of selfishness in a thought, you know it's only an astral/*kamic*(desire) impulse. True intuition – *buddhic* intuition – is always concerned with something unselfish. ***Buddhic* intuition will lead you to higher states of consciousness.**

You've probably heard the expression: "I just know it. I can feel it in my 'gut'." This is <u>false</u> intuition. It <u>might</u> give you the right answer in a given situation, but it's not the intuition we're talking about with true soul intuition. Here's why:

The cerebrosinal system emerges from the mental body. The sympathetic nervous system comes from the astral body. These two systems connect in the solar plexus center. Thoughts and emotions are linked together.

The solar plexus is sometimes referred to as the "abdominal brain." This is the realm of the sense-bound mind, or ego consciousness. It's hard to imagine the "mind" being in the abdominal region below the diaphragm, but that's where it expresses itself (through the solar plexus center).

Intuition from the sense bound mind is "gut" intuition. It comes from the thoughts and emotions of your mental and astral bodies lurking in your subconscious mind – your personality. Your thoughts and emotions tell you what you want to hear, which might not necessarily be the truth. **It's your ego telling you what you want to believe.**

I often use the term: elevate and expand your consciousness. To avoid being misleading, let me explain. You could say **elevating** your consciousness is moving your consciousness from the lower *chakras*/force centers to the higher c*hakras*. What does that mean? It means your Soul is now expressing itself through the higher force centers. This gives your Soul a different perspective.

You could say by **expanding** your consciousness you're becoming conscious on the higher planes beyond the physical, astral, and mental planes *i.e.* the causal, *Buddhic*, and *Atmic/Nirvanic* planes (to be discussed later).

When your conscious awareness is on the higher planes, the Soul is in touch with its true faculties – *buddhi* intelligence, discriminative wisdom and intuition and not governed by the sense mind/ego/personality. So, you could say you moved from a contracted state of consciousness to an expanded state of consciousness.

Ultimately, elevating and expanding your consciousness are two different ways of saying the same thing. In fact, some sources equate each *chakra* with a particular plane of consciousness. Starting with the lowest state of consciousness in the coccygeal/root *chakra* up to the highest state of consciousness in the Crown *chakra*. I can't claim to fully *grok*/grasp this idea, but I'm workin' on it.

The ancient *Hermetic* axiom states: "As above, so below." The seven dimensions/planes of Consciousness in nature are reflected in the seven *chakras* of man (excluding the splenic center because it's not a center of Consciousness). Man is a microcosm of the Universe– the Macrocosm.

So now, when I say elevating and expanding your consciousness, you'll know what I'm talking about.

To expand your consciousness, you don't project it outwards to experience higher dimensions.* When you project outwards, you're only immersing yourself deeper into sense-mind consciousness. The sense-bound mind is limited to the physical dimension/plane – the lowest level of consciousness. You would actually be contracting your consciousness.

*Remember: the dimensions we're talking about are planes of consciousness and nature. Not the intellectual dimensional constructs of philosophy, mathematics, and physics.

To expand your consciousness into higher dimensions of awareness, you withdraw inwards, often called "going within." Sounds kinda counter intuitive. Remember: the physical plane is the lowest dimension (lowest frequency/vibrational rate), emanating <u>outwards</u> from the Solar *Logos*. You want to move your consciousness <u>inwards</u> and upwards to the higher planes/dimensions of causal, *Buddhic*, and *Nirvanic* consciousness, *i.e.* towards the Solar *Logos*.

This is a passive act– being-ness, not doing-ness. Fortunately, the only thing you have to do is still your mind, calm your emotions, and detach from sense-mind consciousness. This is what happens in deep meditation. It can also happen by sun gazing. Relax. Let go. Sun gaze as discussed in the techniques section. Divine Light manifesting as *Prana* imbued with Love and Wisdom will do it for you, **if you let it**.

Soul Control

Just because you move from sense-bound mind consciousness to soul consciousness doesn't mean you withdraw from physical reality. You're still aware of your physical surroundings. It's just you're no longer attached and identified with the physical world. You still function normally, going about your business and helping others evolve spiritually.

Annihilation of the ego, or dissolving egoity, doesn't mean "you" cease to exist. It means the personality/ego is guided by the Soul – a much higher state of consciousness – soul consciousness.*

You don't turn into a mindless zombie with no personality. <u>It means you're no longer **controlled** by emotions, random thoughts, whims, prejudices, and desires.</u> **You don't take things personally.** You remain detached – in the world but not part of it. You're positive, calm, and serene – guided by the discriminative wisdom and intuition of the Soul.

Detached doesn't mean you don't care about anybody or anything. You're just not emotionally involved or identified. Instead of getting all sad and depressed over someone's misfortune or suffering, you maintain your highest state of unconditional love and pour out compassion and sympathy to elevate <u>their</u> state of consciousness.

You realize your purpose in life (as it is for everyone) is to deal with your *karma* and what Divine Will/*Shakti* throws at you. Life's challenges are the lessons you need to learn. You're gonna have to work out your *karma* sooner or later. Might as well get started.

You're just playing a role – your *karmic* role. You don't get depressed, angry, or sad. You always remain in a state of joy, equipoise, and equanimity – not reacting to every little thing that comes up. You're always lighthearted, positive, and upbeat – not negative, sullen, or morose. Might as well enjoy yourself. **Be happy.**

*soul consciousness is only the first step, but it's a **big** step. The ego is all that separates us from God. Technically, annihilation of the ego means you've merged your consciousness directly with God– non-duality.

If you live in the body without being identified with it, no temptations or attachments will keep you tied to the body. It's only when the Soul thinks of itself as the ego/personality that you become body identified. That's why intuition, concentration*, inner perception, calmness, and self-control must be awakened to fight the forces of the pseudo-soul, or ego.

Even after realizing soul consciousness, you can again be drawn into body consciousness by remnants of desires, attachments, and *karma*. It's all part of the process. Don't give up! Each time you experience the state of soul and higher states of consciousness, you're working towards becoming a "Sun of God."

<u>When you're in sense-bound mind, or ego,</u>
<u>consciousness, the ego is **large** and in charge.</u>

<u>When you're in soul, or super, consciousness, the Soul is in control.</u>

*Here, concentration refers to paying attention to what you're thinking, feeling, and doing. Being Self-aware.

Part V

Spiritual Energy Dynamics

*"Now, it's time to explain how subtle psychology, the force centers, Kundalini, and Prana are all interrelated and involved in the elevation and expansion of consciousness. **Are you ready?**"*

author

The Heart Center – the Gateway

To shift from ego consciousness to soul consciousness, we need to move from consciousness in the lower force centers to consciousness in the higher force centers.* From the centers below the diaphragm to the centers above the diaphragm. To pinpoint it, we need to move consciousness from the solar plexus to the heart center and higher centers. Why?

The consciousness of a person under the influence of the sense mind is strongly concentrated in the three lower centers (coccygeal/root, sacral, solar plexus). These centers control body-identified sense activity plus the entire skin surface, the sense organs, and the nerve forces in the physical brain and spinal plexuses. **This is the realm of ego and personality.**

When your stuck in these lower centers, Lower *Manas* comes under the influence of *Kama*. One becomes identified with the gross senses and material desires. This is when sense-bound ego consciousness prevails. Here, you're ruled by your sense-bound mind/ego. **Your consciousness is in a contracted state.**

*When I say Consciousness is in the lower or higher centers, I mean the Soul is expressing itself through those particular centers. There is only one Consciousness (the Soul). The apparent difference is caused by the limitations of the various centers and vehicles. **consciousness is the level of your conscious awareness**

The lower self/ego is not a separate being. It's the Soul putting itself into the personality (mental and astral bodies/spirit/subtle body) to experience the mental, astral and physical planes.

The Soul cannot express itself in the lower planes without being influenced by the personality. Only the purified personality can reflect the Soul accurately. Then, the "Light of the Soul" will shine forth.

On the other hand, when one's consciousness is in the heart, cervical/throat, and medulla* centers, it's under the influence of _buddhi_ intelligence and Soul intuition. Lower _Manas_ is under the control of Upper _Manas_ rather than _Kama_. The senses are now governed by the Soul and its discriminative wisdom. **This is the realm of soul consciousness – an expanded state.**

Now, the Soul can experience and express itself in the world of matter <u>as well as</u> the realm of Spirit. **You live in the realization of your essential unity with your fellows and God.** This is what we're shootin' for. **Your consciousness is in an expanded state. You've moved from ego consciousness to soul consciousness.**

When the Soul expresses itself through the heart center**, it radiates the soul qualities of unconditional love, compassion, and selflessness. When the heart center is open, it becomes a channel for Divine Light and Love.***

*Remember to consider the medulla and the "Spiritual Eye" as a working unit. Some sources say the <u>subtle</u> medulla **is** the "Spiritual Eye."

**Technically, this happens in _Buddhic_ consciousness. We'll get to this in a bit.

***Laughter opens the heart center. Anger closes it.

The "Knot of the Heart"

Okay. We want to shift from sense-bound mind ego consciousness to soul consciousness. That's the plan. How do we do that? Well, there are several factors involved. First, we have to purify the personality (astral and mental bodies). By this, I mean burnin'/breaking up the negative thought-emotion forms and their consequent *samskaras*. Remember: *samskaras* are habitual/chronic thought-emotion forms.

Some negative thought-emotion forms are: selfishness, jealousy, anger, quick temper, hatred, deceitfulness, arrogance, pride, haughtiness, bitterness, and resentment. These thoughts and emotions mostly arise from unfulfilled desire and fear – fear of loneliness and isolation which comes from the false belief of separation between you, your fellows, and the Divine. This is the root of ego consciousness.*

These negative thought-emotion forms habitually dwell in the solar plexus center. They form what is called the "knot of the heart." This knot is referred to as the *vishnu granthi*** in the Eastern Teachings. Some sources describe this knot <u>in</u> the heart center while others suggest it's in the solar plexus center. Others say it lies between the solar plexus center and the heart center. Doesn't really matter.

*This is why fear destroys true soul intuition.

**There are two other *granthis*. The *brahma granthi*, located in the root *chakra*, traps *Kundalini* in the root and sacral *chakras*. This area is involved with instinctual behavior such as survival, the urge to procreate, and instant gratification. People stuck in these centers are often selfish, greedy, power-hungry egomaniacs with no concern or empathy towards others. Fortunately, in most people, this knot is already open.

The *rudra granthi* is said to be in the "Spiritual Eye" or between it and the heart or throat *chakra*. When this *granthi* is opened, *Kundalini* can rise to the highest centers of consciousness in the "Spiritual Eye" and Crown *chakras*. Here, the personal ego ceases to exist and one experiences the awareness of no separation and a feeling of universal oneness. For more about the *rudra granthi*, see pgs 129,130

The point is, the "knot of the heart" creates a psychic blockage in the *Sushumna* (the etheric and subtle channel for subtle energy that runs between the root *chakra* and the Crown *chakra*) which keeps the awakened *Kundalini** from going to the higher centers and elevating and expanding your consciousness.

If the awakened *Kundalini* is trapped in the lower centers (below the diaphragm), it will intensify the personality, increase selfishness, and trap one in the sense-bound mind and ego consciousness with often disastrous consequences. That's why this knot must be pierced/loosened/eliminated.**

To open the knot so *Kundalini* can rise to the heart center and higher, you must replace the negative thoughts and emotions with selflessness, unconditional love, compassion, kindness, humility, gentleness, tolerance, truthfulness, joy, peace and realization of unity with each other and the Divine/God/Consciousness.

How do you do that? **Read on!**

* *Kundalini* is related to consciousness. Soon to be explained.

**Careful consideration will suggest the "knot of the heart," *Kama*, Lower *Manas*, and Upper *Manas* are all related to *Kundalini*

Force Center Dynamics and Consciousness

The force centers are said to be swirling vortices of *Prana* (not structures themselves) which connect the vehicles/bodies of the Soul – the causal, mental, astral bodies – with each other and to the Etheric Double and the dense physical body.

The *chakras* also absorb and distribute *Prana* to the etheric body and thence to the physical body, thus keeping these bodies alive. There are several varieties of *Prana*, all of which are present in all the *chakras*, but in each *chakra*, one of the varieties is always greatly predominate.*

The centers originate in the subtle spine (*Sushumna*), where they interface with the physical nervous system by way of the *Nadis*. A stalk-like channel of energy connects the spinal center to the anterior surface of the Etheric Double where the flower bell-like part of the *chakra is* located. The spinal center, the stalk, and the flower bell are all part of a force center.

The *chakras* are perpetually rotating, and into the open mouth of each flows *Prana*. *Prana* pours into each center and redirects at right angles (in line with the surface of the body) giving the appearance of the bell of a flower. This is one way the force center is vitalized. (See next chapter)

The flow of vitality through a force center is separate and distinct from its development brought about by the awakening of *Kundalini*. When *Kundalini* starts moving up the *Sushumna*, it travels outward along the stalk of the force center towards the flower bell on the anterior surface and meets the incoming *Prana* (divine life).

*By **no** means do I claim to know everything about how force centers work. I wish somebody could/would tell me. I'm merely putting together some things I've learned in an attempt to explain the process of spiritual transformation by sun gazing.

There, *Prana* and *Kundalini* grind together, revolve in opposite directions, and create considerable pressure. The resulting compound energy vivifies the plexuses and awakens them as centers of Consciousness.

What does *Kundalini* have to do with our level of consciousness? Somehow, when *Kundalini* and *Prana* interact, they create a place for Consciousness to be/happen. That's the best way I can put it. Just remember: Consciousness follows *Kundalini*.

Put another way: **Primordial Creative Force (*Kundalini*) and Creative Intelligent Life Force (*Prana*) meet for Consciousness to express itself.** When all the *chakras* are awakened and *Kundalini* rises to the upper *chakras*, one experiences/realizes soul consciousness, *Buddhic* consciousness and the non-duality* of *Nirvanic* consciousness.

***Kundalini* energy is the foundation of our consciousness. When *Kundalini* moves up and down the *Sushumna*, our consciousness moves with it.**

***Kundalini* enters the human body at the root *chakra*. There, *Kundalini* and *Prana* merge and give life and consciousness to the central and sympathetic nervous systems resulting in body awareness/ consciousness. When the *Kundalini* is blocked by the "knot of the heart," consciousness remains in the lower centers resulting in body identified ego consciousness.**

Prana from sun gazing **can** vivify the centers, but if the heart center is closed/blocked – *Kundalini* can't rise through the *Sushumna* and awaken the higher *chakras* as centers of consciousness. That's why we have to open the heart center. How do we do that? **By purifying the spirit/subtle body.**

*Non-duality refers to the essential One-ness of God, man, and all of Creation. Non-duality is the state of consciousness realized in *Nirvana*.

Vitality Absorption

Before we get to spirit purification, I'd like to explain how *Prana* vitalizes the Etheric Double and the dense physical body.

On the physical plane (including the etheric plane), *Prana* emanates from the sun. When there's plenty of sunshine, there's plenty of *Prana*. *Prana* enters some physical "atoms"* and greatly energizes them, making them animated and glowing. Here's what happens.

When *Prana* from a higher dimension (astral plane) wells up within one of these atoms, the atom is vitalized and attracts around itself six other atoms (filled with various frequencies [colors] of *Prana*) and forms a "Vitality Globule." (Not the most elegant word)

These globules manifest on the highest subdivision of the etheric plane (part of the physical plane).** They are the vital life force of the Etheric Double and the dense physical body. This is a type of specific *Prana*.

While the force (*Prana*) vivifying these globules isn't physical sunlight, it manifests through sunlight. These globules are brilliant and sparkling and can be seen in the atmosphere. They are almost colorless and shine with a white or slightly golden light.

*Not the physical atoms of modern science, but rather the basic type of "matter" in the highest sub-plane of the physical plane – sometimes called "ultimate physical atoms" in the occult tradition.

**Remember: the physical plane consists of solids, liquids, and gases along with four distinct etheric sub-planes of varying vibrational rates. We're referring to the highest plane (highest vibrational rate) of the four etheric sub-planes – adjacent to the lowest sub-plane of the astral plane. Got that? (humor)

On a bright sunny day, try looking directly away from the sun and focus your eyes a few feet away from yourself with the clear sky in the background. You'll see them flashing. You might actually be able to hear them popping or ringing. You can also see them on overcast days while facing the sun, when there aren't so many of them and they can be more easily distinguished against a darker background.

The splenic, or **Surya** (sun), *chakra** absorbs the Vitality Globules from the atmosphere. The Vitality Globules are drawn into the splenic center, where they're broken up into seven component atoms, each charged with one of seven varieties of *Prana*.

Inconveniently, the divisions do not correspond to the colors of the visible physical electromagnetic solar spectrum (like the rainbow) but are like the colors seen on higher levels in the causal, mental, astral, and etheric bodies – colors seen by clairvoyants.

These atoms are then caught up by the rotating secondary forces and spun around the *chakra*. From there, the *Prana* charged atoms are distributed to the other force centers of the etheric and astral bodies through *Nadis* (luminous channels of energy).

There, the charge of *Prana* is withdrawn from them like a charge of electricity might be withdrawn. The *Prana* gives life to the Etheric Double and through that to the physical body, directly affecting the health of the body. This is how normal life function is energized by the *chakras*.

Once the atoms discharge their *Prana*, they're eventually dispersed in all directions through the Etheric Double and the pores of the skin. A person of high vitality has more of these *Prana* charged particles than he needs and is a source of vitality to those around him. On the other hand, someone of low vitality can drain vitality from others.

*The *chakra* that's not a center of Consciousness. When it's energized, the *Surya chakra* appears radiant, glowing, and sun-like.

Note: Of most importance to us, the heart center receives the yellow ray from the splenic center and sends it to to the core of the crown *chakra*.

The "Spiritual Eye"

Although it's directly related to sun gazing practice, I placed this chapter here because an understanding of some subtle psychology is necessary to fully understand it. In the sun gazing instructions, it was suggested, while sun gazing, to gently focus your gaze toward the bridge of the nose – the location of the subtle "Spiritual Eye." Here's why:

The subtle medulla, while not normally recognized as a force center, does play an important role in consciousness. The subtle medulla is where Consciousness (as the Soul) enters the **physical** body.

The subtle *Ida* and *Pingala Nadis*, which interface with the sympathetic chain on either side of the spinal cord, originate in the coccygeal center and terminate in the subtle **medulla**. These *Nadis*, which connect at the solar plexus, are involved with thought, sensation, and emotion and give us sense-mind body consciousness.

The subtle medulla is also connected to the "Spiritual Eye" – the subtle center where Consciousness, as the Soul, enters the **subtle** body. The "Spiritual Eye" is also known as the center of Christ/*Buddhic* Consciousness. (More on this later)

So, the subtle medulla is where your consciousness expresses itself as Soul or ego. You could consider the subtle medulla as a switch that directs your conscious awareness either to the lower centers and outwards as sense-mind body consciousness or inwards as soul consciousness in the subtle medulla and the higher centers of consciousness in the "Spiritual Eye" and the Crown *chakra*.

From the perspective of spiritual psychology, the subtle medulla center seems to be where Lower and Upper *Manas* struggle. Where ego/personality and Soul fight for control.

Kama (material desire) is in the coccygeal center – the main channel of outflowing life force (*Prana*) and Consciousness. Pulled by *Kama*, Lower *Manas* (the mind) becomes immersed in sense-mind, or ego, consciousness.

On the other hand, the Soul's *buddhi* intelligence draws consciousness inwards towards soul consciousness. Lower *Manas*, under the influence of *buddhi* intelligence from Upper *Manas*, breaks away from *Kama*. The personality/ego is now governed by the discriminative wisdom and intuition of the Soul seeking soul consciousness and beyond rather than the desire for sense gratification driven by *Kama*.

Remember: soul consciousness is the Soul acting through Upper *Manas* in the causal body governed by *buddhi* intelligence, not diminished by the personality/ego of Lower *Manas* in the mental body manipulated by *Kama*.

When Consciousness (Soul) and *Prana* (life force) are engaged in looking at duality through the two eyes, you become body conscious. When you withdraw your Consciousness and life force from the two eyes and gather them together to be concentrated at one point in the "Spiritual Eye" at the bridge of your nose, you have the "single eye" vision of soul consciousness.

"The light of the body is the eye: therefore, if thine eye be single, thy whole body shall be full of light." *

So, when you gently direct your gaze towards the point between the eyebrows while sun gazing, the dual currents of life force (*Prana*) and Consciousness flowing outward from the medulla reunite into one current flowing inwards towards the "Spiritual Eye." The Soul and the ego are united.

One is now free from sensory distractions and emotional likes and dislikes – **detachment. You're in a state of soul consciousness. It should be noted this probably won't happen the first time you sun gaze (it might), but after continued practice, it will.**

*Matthew 6:22

Gently aiming your gaze on the point between the two eyes during sun gazing **and/or** meditation helps keep one's eyes neither fully closed nor fully opened – "half mast". The dividing line between the upper darkness and the lower material light of half closed eyes is called the "horizon of super (soul) consciousness."

If you fix your gaze on this horizon at the point between the eyebrows, where darkness and light meet, without straining the eyes, you refocus the two currents in the two eyes into the original single current of Consciousness as Soul in the "Spiritual Eye."

It's important to hold your gaze steady without restless movement of the eyeballs or flickering of the eyelids, which can be a distraction. That's why I recommend slightly moving your head around while sun gazing rather than moving your eyes with your ocular muscles.

Slowly and rhythmically blinking your eyes not only helps keep you from focusing directly on the sun. It will prevent your eyelids from twitching. It also puts you into a gentle rhythm and calms you down. After some practice, all this is done automatically without any thinking or distraction. **Blink faster if you need to.**

Repeat: I strongly recommend gently aiming your gaze (without straining) toward the spot at the bridge of your nose and relaxing your eyelids to half mast while sun gazing. **Not only does it make it a lot easier to sun gaze. It's a big factor in experiencing an elevated and expanded state of consciousness.**

If you go "within" by directing your gaze at the spot between the eyebrows, shifting from outward consciousness through the lower centers, inward to the higher centers of the "Spiritual Eye" and Crown *chakras*, you can experience *Buddhic* and *Atmic/Nirvanic* consciousness. How?

Remember the *rudra granthi* – the knot blocking *Kundalini* from rising to the "Spiritual Eye" and Crown *chakras*? By focusing your eyes at the spot between your eyes while sun gazing or meditating, your conscious awareness is directed away from the lower centers towards the highest centers. From outward and lower to inward and higher.

There's a breaking away from the sense of individuality in soul consciousness and the realization of unity, first in *Buddhic* consciousness, then fully in *Atmic/Nirvanic* consciousness. So, <u>perhaps</u> this is how you open the *rudra granthi*.

There's a lot more to the "Spiritual Eye" worth getting into, but that's way beyond the scope of this book and my knowledge, which is about sun gazing for spiritual transformation by purification of the subtle body/spirit.

Note: You can/should use this same practice while meditating after sun gazing or meditating at anytime of the day. Concentrating the light of the two eyes at the point between the two eyebrows, at the origin of the nose, is a prime requisite of *kyiya* yoga meditation. It **will** expand and elevate your consciousness. Try blinking with or without your eyes closed while you're at it, if you like.*

*You'll have to try this before it makes any sense.

Part VI

Purification

"The prime secret of alchemical transmutation is an inner mystery – the purgation and perfection of the subtle embodiment [of the Soul].

They [alchemists] sought the soul-freeing doctrine of regeneration."

From: *The Doctrine of the Subtle Body in Western Tradition*

by G R S Mead

*"The Soul is already perfect – made in the Image of God. The spirit limits the expression of the Soul. This book is about **spirit--ual** transformation. **Spiritual transformation takes place in the subtle body/spirit.** In order to experience spiritual transformation, at least in a positive manner, one must <u>purify</u> one's thoughts (mental body) and emotions (astral body) i.e. the subtle body/spirit. When the spirit is purified, the 'Light of the Soul' shines through. That's what being 'born again in spirit' means."*

author

Purification of the Subtle Body

When purifying the subtle body,* what gets purified? The negative thoughts and emotions ingrained in the mental and astral bodies. They need to be broken up and replaced by positive thoughts and emotions.

What do we mean by negative thoughts and emotions? Any thought or emotion contrary to your or your fellow's spiritual evolution is negative – any thought or emotion that leads to contraction, separation, or dissolution. Any thought or emotion leading to selfishness, jealousy, anger, hatred, greed, arrogance, pride, and haughtiness.

The idea you're better than someone else, more spiritual, more important, or more worthy. The belief you have the right to harm someone else to get what you want. Any thought or emotion that closes the heart center and traps you in ego-bound contracted consciousness, separating you from your true Divine nature.

Remember: thoughts and emotions are vibrating energy patterns of subtle matter in the spirit. When you harbor these thoughts and emotions for a long time, they can become fixed – almost permanent. They cause you to think, feel, and act in a predetermined way.

Called *samskaras*, these thought-emotion forms are fixed prejudices, opinions, likes, dislikes, beliefs, reactions, perceptions, aversions, and attractions. There are positive and negative s*amskaras*. Most people have some of both. We want to get rid of the negative *samskaras* and the negative thoughts and emotions that cause them.

*Remember: for our purposes, we equate the subtle body with the spirit and personality because all three involve the mental and astral bodies.

Let's take a closer look at the nature of thoughts and emotions. They can be divided into two groups: Love and Hate.

Love is the force of attraction to bring about Unity – the very nature of Love. Love is expressed by sympathy, self-sacrifice, and the desire to give (charity). Sympathy is feeling for another as one would feel for oneself. Self-sacrifice is a recognition of the need of another as your own need.

Giving is the action of the Soul. Love is the nature and essence of the Soul. Compassion, kindness, sympathy, respect, love, benevolence, harmony, tolerance, patience, humility, reverence, gratitude, and under-standing are all qualities of Love. **Love is Unity.**

On the other hand, Hate is the force of repulsion driving one apart from another. Hate is characterized by antipathy, self-aggrandizement, and desire to take. Hate is lack of concern/empathy for others, being self-serving, and selfish. Hate is taking for oneself rather than giving to others. Hate works through the ego/pseudo-soul. **Hate's nature is separateness and isolation.**

Some qualities of Hate are scorn, condescension, jealousy, cruelty, arrogance, quick-temperedness, selfishness, greed, anger, combativeness, violence, aggressiveness, insolence, intolerance, haughtiness, spitefulness and lack of patience. Hate looking upwards is fear. Hate looking downwards is scorn. Hate between equals is desire for mutual injury.

According to clairvoyants who can see thought-emotion forms, those of a higher vibrational rate – those of expansive soul consciousness and higher states – congregate in the upper part of the mental and astral bodies above the diaphragm. Thoughts and feelings of Love express through the heart center.

Conversely, coarse heavy feelings and thoughts of a lower vibrational rate – those of contracted ego consciousness – linger below the diaphragm. Thoughts and feelings of Hate express through the solar plexus.

The gateway to soul consciousness and higher states is through the heart center. The "knot of the heart," between the solar plexus chakra and the heart *chakra*, is the subtle energy blockage that prevents *Kundalini* from rising to the higher centers and elevating and expanding consciousness. The knot, itself, is the negative *samskaras* trapping one in ego consciousness.

So, we need to break up the negative *samskaras* creating the blockage – the "knot of the heart." How do we do that? By replacing the negative thoughts and emotions of ego consciousness with the positive thoughts and emotions of soul consciousness and higher states. Okay, how do we do that?

When you experience the higher thoughts and emotions of soul consciousness and higher states of consciousness, you create positive vibrations in the mental and astral bodies, at least, temporarily. These vibrations override the lower thoughts and emotions causing ego consciousness and replace them with the higher thoughts and emotions of soul consciousness, *Buddhic* consciousness and *Nirvanic* consciousness.

In other words, the negative vibrating energy patterns are broken up and replaced with positive vibrating energy patterns. By a process of sympathetic vibration, the mental and astral bodies (your spirit) are purified of negative thoughts and emotions. In short, you're reprogramming your personality/spirit.

When you're in a higher state of consciousness, you're at a higher vibrational rate. At least temporarily, the lower thoughts and emotions of the ego – vibrating energy patterns of astral and mental matter – are replaced by the higher thoughts and emotions of the Soul. The "knot of the heart" is opened. For a while, at least, you're in a state of soul consciousness or higher rather than ego consciousness.

Unfortunately, after a time, the aberrated thoughts and emotions often rear their ugly little heads. It would seem the "matter" of the astral and mental bodies has "memory," and the *samskaras* reform. This causes the knot to "tighten," resulting in the "flip-flop." You drop out of soul consciousness back into ego consciousness.

But, fear not. With the continued spiritual practice of sun gazing and/or meditation, you can eventually replace the negative vibes with higher vibes. That's how you purify the subtle body/spirit.

When you're in ego consciousness, you harbor these negative thoughts and emotions because you are identified with your ego rather than the Soul. You live in a state of isolation and separateness, cut off from your fellows and the Divine. You see others as your enemies – in the way of getting what you want.

When you're in soul consciousness (not driven by *kama*), you're resistant to negative thoughts and emotions because you're identified with the Soul whose essence is Divine Love and Unity. You see others as your brothers and sisters – all working together for the common good.

The first step is to get out of ego consciousness and into soul consciousness. After that, you can eventually expand to *Buddhic*/Christ consciousness where unity with all souls is experienced. Ultimately, you **realize** *Nirvana* – a state of non-duality – where you, everyone, all of Creation, and God are all One – Consciousness. (More on that soon)

By now, the discerning reader has probably noticed I've presented a bit of a catch 22 situation. I've basically said the best way to get into soul consciousness is to be in soul consciousness. So, the question remains: how does one get into soul consciousness?

The short answer is: **Open the "knot of the heart."** * **Purify the *Nadis*, particularly the *Ida, Pingala*, and *Sushumna*. Awaken Kundalini.** This is not necessarily a step-by-step procedure. Things will be happening simultaneously as well as sequentially. The good news is you don't have to really think about it. **You just do the techniques in the proper manner with the correct attitude and let the Divine Love and Wisdom imbued within *Prana* manifesting through the sun do it for you.**

*Opening the heart center and loosening, or piercing, the "knot of the heart" are the same process for our purposes.

What Does Sun Gazing Have To Do With It?

Well, now comes the <u>big</u> **Question–?**. **How can sun gazing open up the heart center? <u>By attuning to Divine Love while practicing the Attunement-Reflection Technique.</u>** Let's explain how this works.

Consciousness/Absolute Spirit/God manifests in Creation as a Cosmic Vibration which expresses Itself as Cosmic Sound <u>and</u> Cosmic Light. This Vibration is called the Solar *Logos*. *OM* is the sound of the Solar *Logos*. The Spiritual Sun is the Light of the Solar *Logos*.

Prana - an emanation of the Solar *Logos* - is the link between Absolute Spirit (God) and matter. Existing on all planes and sub-planes, *Prana* is the Creative Intelligent Life Force that created and sustains the universe. On the physical plane, including the etheric plane, *Prana* comes through the sun along with physical light and the rest of the electromagnetic spectrum.

<u>Imbued within *Prana* are Divine Love and Wisdom. Divine Love is the expression, or feeling, of Absolute Spirit in manifestation as Vibratory Creation. Divine Love "is" Ultimate Reality. Divine Love is unconditional, unlimited, universal, nonjudgmental, non-expecting, all embracing, all forgiving.</u>

.

When sun gazing, *Prana*, imbued with Divine Love and Wisdom, pours into your "Spiritual Eye" (brow *chakra* – center at the bridge of the nose) and projects to the subtle medulla, also known as the "mouth of God." From the medulla center, *Prana* floods the subtle body (including the Etheric Double) and all the force centers with Divine Light and Love. All the centers resonate with the *OM*, putting you in harmony with the Song of the Solar *Logos*.

So, the Word of God is Divine Love which manifests as Light (*Prana*) through the physical sun. It is this Divine Love which we <u>attune</u> to while sun gazing. Once we are attuned to Divine Love, we become mirrors, <u>reflecting</u> Divine Love to all of creation and back to God. You will experience harmony, peace, bliss, and unity.

The key to practicing the Attunement-Reflection Technique successfully is to surrender your <u>s</u>elf will to Divine Will – the force driving and guiding our spiritual evolution. That's why we should be without selfishness, desire, expectation, demand, guile, prejudice, or anger. Especially while sun gazing.

We seek not to express <u>our</u> will, but rather Divine Will, which is Love. You're not trying to project yourself anywhere. You're not trying to do anything intentionally. Surrender to Divine Will/*Shakti*. In order to do that, you must be detached. **Let go!**

Vrittis (whirlpools) are alternating waves of thoughts, desires, and emotions arising from likes and dislikes produced by the contact of the mind with the senses. Similar to the "wild horse of the mind" in *Buddhism*. When constantly repeated, they become *samskaras* (permanent prejudices) which in turn create more *vrittis* which ceaselessly arise and subside in the conscious mind.

In order to hear the "Voice of the Soul," the mind must be still – unshaken by outward things. You must have no desires and aversions. It is only when personal desires and aversions have ceased to exist that the mind will be able to hear the "Voice of the Soul" with it's *buddhi* intelligence, discriminative wisdom, and intuition.

When you're thoughts and emotions are calm and still while sun gazing and/or meditating, you become detached from the desires of *Kama Manas* driven by body attachment and sensory gratification, fears of non-fulfillment of those desires, and anger when those desires are unfulfilled. That's what detachment is really all about. Breaking free of the sense-mind bound ego driven by *Kama* (material desire).

Instead of obeying the screamin' bellowings of the *Kama* driven ego, you follow the gentle whisperings of the Soul and its *buddhi* intelligence, discriminative wisdom, and intuition. **You shift from contracted ego consciousness to expanded states of consciousness.**

So, just relax, let go, and harmonize with the Divine Love vibration. Still the mind and emotions. Breathe easily, slowly, and rhythmically. Eventually, you'll be able to hear and feel the beat of your spiritual heart. There you go. Get the rhythm. Become a living expression of Divine Love.

<u>Tune in Turn on Be the Love Feel the Bliss</u>

<u>This opens the "knot of the heart." This puts you in an expanded and elevated state of consciousness – soul consciousness and beyond. You become one with Spirit, the Universe, everyone, and everything. Your spirit is purified by Divine Love.</u>

This is the true *Agape* – the outpouring of God's Love filling your open heart. This Love is love of the highest form – Love of God for man and Love of man for God. It's an all embracing Love – a universal and **unconditional love** that transcends and persists regardless of circumstances.

<u>Selfless, Self-sacrificing, and Charitable</u>

Love looking downwards is benevolence. Love looking upwards is reverence. Love between you and your fellows is Brotherhood.

"You shall love the Lord your God with all your heart and with all your soul and with all your mind." This is the great and first commandment. And the second is: "You shall love your neighbor as yourself."

Agape is translated as love or charity. It also represents the Communal Meal of Fellowship of the *Essenes* and their successors – the first Christians. These mystics gathered at dawn, faced the rising sun, and let Divine Light, imbued with Divine Love and Divine Wisdom, heal their spirits and nourish their Souls. Then, they reflected that Divine Light back to the sun for the benefit of all Creation. As did like-minded communities around the world.

Now, you know how they did it.

We can do it too.

Remember: the essence of the Soul is Divine Love. When you're in soul consciousness and beyond, you're an expression of that Divine Love.

Love is Peace, Harmony, and Unity.

Purifying the *Nadis*

In the etheric, subtle, and causal bodies, *Prana* flows through a complex and extensive network of fixed pathways called *Nadis*. This network is sometimes referred to as the *pranic* sheath, or the *pranamaya kosha*. The word *Nadi* has been roughly translated as a "river of energy in motion."

The *Nadis* are not organized structures of matter – they're channels, or streams, of energy (*Prana*). It's commonly stated there are 72,000 *Nadis* spread throughout the body, with some estimates exceeding 300,000.

Fortunately, we are mostly concerned with the three major *Nadis*: *Ida*, *Pingala*, and *Sushumna*. The *Ida* and *Pingala* surround and interpenetrate the two long sympathetic ganglionic chains that parallel the spinal cord – one on each side. The *Sushumna* surrounds and interpenetrates the spinal cord. The *Ida* and *Pingala* originate in the root *chakra* and terminate in the medulla. The *Sushumna* originates in the root *chakra* and terminates in the Crown *chakra*.

The rest of the *Nadis* originate from two sources: a little below the navel (solar plexus *chakra*) and around the heart center. There's that "above and below the diaphragm thing" again. At various points within the etheric and subtle bodies, these *Nadis* intersect and form the *chakras* – plexuses of subtle energy. Remember: *Prana* interfaces the physical nervous system with the astral and mental bodies and distributes vitality to the physical body.

The *Ida*, *Pingala*, and *Sushumna* conduct energy from the *chakras* situated along the spinal column to all the other *Nadis*. Maximum *pranic* charges flow through them, and they impact the entire network instantaneously. They're the main channels for distribution of energy throughout the *pranic* network. They govern the whole system of *Nadis* and all the bodily processes.

There's a very close connection between the *Nadis* and the body, between the body and the subtle body (mental and astral bodies), between the subtle body and *Prana*, and between *Prana* and *Kundalini*. Purification of the *Nadis* is a major factor in purifying the physical body, Etheric Double, and spirit (subtle body).

When the *Nadis* are purified, *Prana* (Creative Intelligent Life Force) can work freely in the physical and subtle body of a person. The purification of the *Nadis* (streams of *Prana*) facilitates the ascent of the *Kundalini*.

Any impurities impede it's ascent. Without the awakening/ascent of *Kundalini*, you won't be able to expand and elevate to soul consciousness, Christ, or *Buddhic,* Consciousness /*Salvilalpa Samadhi*, and Cosmic Consciousness/ *Nirvana*/ *Nirvikalpa Samadhi*/ Self-Realization/ *Gnosis*. (these states of consciousness are all related)

How do you purify your *Nadis*? The most common spiritual practices are: *kriya* yoga, *pranayama*, *kundalini* yoga, fasting, meditation, visualization, and prayer. A much quicker way is:

"Sun Gazing"! In the proper manner with the correct attitude, of course. Particularly, the Attunement-Reflection Technique and the Crown Technique. *Prana* – Creative Intelligent Life Force – will enter through the etheric matter of the eye as well as all the chakras, particularly the "Spiritual Eye," the Crown Chakra, and Heart Center, and purify the *Nadis*. Divine Light and Love will "illuminate" all the vehicles of the Soul.

Awakening *Kundalini*

Remember: the *Nadis* form the *chakras*, so when you're purifying them, you're also purifying and energizing the *chakras*. But energizing the *chakras* is not necessarily elevating and expanding your consciousness. To do that, the "knot of the heart" must be loosened and *Kundalini* must be awakened. We've already explained how to release the "knot of the heart" and purify the *Nadis*. Time to explain how *Kundalini* is awakened.

The static, unmanifested, or dormant, *Kundalini* resides in the root *chakra*. It's coiled up and blocks the entrance of the *Sushumna* at the base of the spine. The *Sushumna* remains closed unless *Kundalini* is awakened.

The various techniques of *Kundalini* yoga previously mentioned move *Prana* in the *Ida* and *Pingala* down to the base of the spine where *Kundalini* is coiled. There, the vital energies in the *Ida* and *Pingala* are unified and put into balance, allowing *Kundalini* to **spontaneously** rise up the *Sushumna*, awakening the *chakras* and making them active centers of Consciousness.

Ultimately, that's all there is to it. The *Ida* is associated with control of emotions and *Pingala* with control of thoughts. Purifying the *Ida* and *Pingala Nadis* makes it easier to control thoughts or emotions. And purifying your thoughts and emotions puts the *Ida* and *Pingala* into balance.

Somehow, it's all tied together. So, calming your thoughts and emotions is an important factor in awakening *Kundalini*. Just another reason why it's so important to calm yourself while performing the sun gazing techniques.

Shaktipat is the purposeful transfer of spiritual energy from the higher realms of consciousness by a spiritual master directly to the recipient. It's considered an act of grace conferred by the *guru*. *Shakti* refers to spiritual energy. *Pata* refers to the transmission, or conferring upon, of spiritual energy to one person by another. *Shaktipat* is spiritual energy that awakens *Kundalini*. **That spiritual energy is *Prana*.**

Shaktipat has been called the "the descent of grace." Grace is Divine Love and Wisdom. Grace is effortlessly received. What is achieved by *Shaktipat* is not achieved by doing-ness. It's achieved through grace and being-ness. One has to be ready to receive the energy – ready and willing to transform. The *Shaktipat* does the work. *Shaktipat* works best when thoughts and emotions are still.

Shaktipat dissolves the physical, emotional, intellectual, and spiritual blockages (*vrittis*, *samskaras*, hangups, *karmic* baggage) that we cannot take out ourselves, or would take a long time to clear otherwise. Each time *Shaktipat* happens, a different set of blockages are removed. It's a complete restructuring of the vehicles of the Soul. Without some kind of *Shaktipat*, this would take a very long time.

Shaktipat purifies the *Nadis* – particularly the *Ida*, *Pingala*, and *Sushumna*. It **doesn't** jumpstart *Kundalini* into activity. Needing no push or artificial intervention, *Kundalini* **spontaneously** moves up the *Sushumna* when the *Ida* and *Pingala* are in balance. **Forcefully pushing Kundalini energy with certain techniques can have disastrous consequences if the person is not ready i.e., if the heart center isn't open.** *Shaktipat* **involves no manipulation or forcing.**

Well, what if you don't know a *guru* or other spiritually advanced teacher who can give you *Shaktipat*? I recommend the Crown Technique.

If you think about it, the Crown Technique works in basically the same manner. When you place your right hand slightly above the Crown *chakra*, with your left hand facing the sun (if possible, with a cross or the symbol of the Solar Logos), you're infusing the Crown *chakra* with *Prana* imbued with Divine Love and Wisdom.

The incoming *Prana*, attuned to the frequency of the Solar *Logos* (Divine Love), travels directly down the *Sushumna*, *Ida,* and *Pingala* and purifies them. In fact, the subtle and etheric bodies (including the *Nadis* and *chakras*) are charged with *Prana* – Creative Intelligent Life Force. The slumbering *Kundalini* awakens and rises **spontaneously**, moving you from ego consciousness to soul consciousness and higher.

Consider the Solar *Logos* as your *guru,* giving you spiritual energy (*Shaktipat*). You become the agent of the Solar *Logos,* basically transmitting *Shaktipat* (Spiritual Light) to yourself while doing the Crown Technique. Only, you don't really do anything intentionally.

All you do is direct the *Prana,* imbued with Divine Love and Wisdom, from the Solar *Logos* through the sun to the Crown *chakra.* You could say you're anointing yourself with Divine Light (*Prana*). The *Prana* does the rest. Your job is to relax and let it happen.

Photismos is defined as illumination, or enlightenment, with Light, itself, being the source (beginning) of the illumination. Baptism (Greek – *baptismos*) is purification by immersion in water. You could say *photism* (Greek – *photismos*) is purification of the spirit by immersion in Light.

When you think about it, this is exactly what you're doing with the Crown Technique. In ancient times, oil (oil lamp) was symbolic of light. Anointing with oil was symbolic of anointing with Light. There's usually a deeper meaning behind symbolic rituals, at least at the time they were originally instituted. Incidentally, *Christos* (Greek) and *Messiah* (Hebrew) both mean "anointed one." Gettin' off track here.

In most people, *Kundalini* (at the level of the root *chakra*) and *Prana* in the *Ida* and *Pingala* interact with the cerebrospinal and sympathetic nervous systems to give us body consciousness. That's the center our Consciousness normally works through. Remember: *Kundalini* and *Prana* together give a place for Consciousness (the Soul) to express itself.

With the partial entering of *Kundalini* into the *Sushumna,* the workings of the *Ida* and *Pingala* are diminished, and *Kundalini* begins to move upwards. But as *Kundalini* rises, it often gets stopped at the "knot of the heart," locking us in sense-mind ego consciousness.

When the knot is finally loosened, *Kundalini* can rise to the higher centers (above the diaphragm) and move us into soul consciousness and higher. At this point, the activities of the *Ida* and *Pingala* stop. Admittedly, this is a crude description of a complex matter.

The *Nadis* <u>must</u> be purified, the "knot of the heart" <u>must</u> be opened, and *Kundalini* <u>must</u> rise to the higher centers for the elevation and expansion of consciousness. I believe the Attunement-Reflection Technique and the Crown Technique are the quickest and most efficient means to accomplish this.

Note: It would seem the rising of *Kundalini* to the higher *chakras* is not necessarily a one-shot event. It all depends on the *granthis*/subtle energy blockages in the *Sushumna*, which can open or close according to the state of your thoughts and emotions.*

This can change from moment to moment unless you're paying attention. It's a lifelong process. Even after experiencing elevated and expanded states of consciousness, you can still "backslide." Your *karma* can/will pull you down.**

Another thing to keep in mind is there are different stages of consciousness on each plane. It can take time to rise to the highest sub-planes of a particular plane of Consciousness.

You often have to work your way through the sub-planes by repeatedly realizing a sub-plane before realizing the next sub-plane. It all depends on how responsive you are to the "higher" vibrations of Love and Unity.

*i.e., the purity of your astral and mental bodies must be maintained.

Don't forget. The techniques **are illuminating, but you still have to settle your *karma*. See pgs 173-176 for how that works.

The "Bridge of Light"

Earlier, we mentioned the "Bridge of Light," also known as the *antahkarana*. Basically, this refers to the connection between Upper *Manas* in the causal body and Lower *Manas* in the mental body.* Remember: the human Soul resides in the causal body and sends its vibrations down through the lower bodies to express itself. This is how the Soul governs the personality. (Soul consciousness)

The vehicles of the Soul aren't separate in space. They inter-penetrate each other. They've been described as being joined by innumerable fine "wires," or channels, of light. Every thought, emotion, and action working against soul consciousness and spiritual evolvement puts an unequal strain upon these "wires," twisting and entangling them.

When someone is deeply trapped in sense-bound mind ego consciousness, under the influence of *Kama,* these "wires" become severely entangled and communication between upper *Manas* (Soul) and lower *Manas* (mind) is seriously impeded. As a result, only the personality/ego can influence the brain.

The personality must reflect the "Light of the Soul."** When a force comes down from a higher plane to a lower plane, it's subject to transmutation in the vehicles into which it comes. The transmutation of the force depends on the nature of the vehicle. That's why the personality must be purified.

Remember: The personality, also known as the spirit and/or the ego, is basically the thought-emotion forms in the mental and astral bodies. So, what are we purifying? The fixed prejudices, attitudes, opinions, aberrant thoughts, and distorted emotions commonly known as *samskaras*.

*There's more to the "Bridge of Light," but that's a good enough description for our purposes at the moment.

**Selfishness is an intensification of the personality which distorts that Light.

These thought-emotion forms have been described as whirlpools in the astral and mental bodies. After a period of time, they become "crystallized" into *samskaras* resulting in the "wires," or channels, of light, becoming firmly entangled.

To disentangle these "wires," the whirlpools in the mental and astral bodies must be "combed" out. How do we do that? Countless incarnations will eventually straighten out the distortion. Meditation is the standard practice to reprogram your thoughts and emotions and elevate and expand your consciousness. However, that takes a long time.

A much faster way is to sun gaze in a proper manner with the correct attitude. Particularly the Attunement-Reflection Technique and the Crown Technique. How's that work?

Remember: emanating from the Solar *Logos* is Divine Will manifesting through Divine Light as *Prana,* imbued with Divine Love and Wisdom. Divine Will is the driving force of our spiritual evolution. This Will seeks for all Souls to experience/realize their unity with each other and their own Divinity.

When employing the sun gazing techniques suggested, you tune directly into Divine Will. Your entire being is flooded with Divine Love and Wisdom. You resonate/entrain with Divine Love and Wisdom, purifying all thoughts and emotions leading to actions which oppose your spiritual evolution.

This will break up the whirlpools and straighten out the entanglement of the channels in the subtle body/spirit, thus eliminating the distortion of the Soul's reflection into its lower vehicles.

The channels between the causal and higher bodies of the Soul and the lower bodies of the personality will be opened and widened, allowing the light of the Soul's *buddhi* intelligence, discriminative wisdom, and intuition to reflect clearly on the personality. In other words, the Soul can now guide the personality. This is how you build the "Bridge of Light."

We have a human nature (driven by *Kama*/desire) <u>and</u> a Divine Nature (guided by Divine Will) both struggling for control. Until the Soul gains control of the personality, the ego clings to self-centeredness. When the lower vibrations of the ego are raised and attuned with the vibrations of the Soul, the Soul is in control.

This is often referred to as the mystical "Divine Marriage" because the Soul and the ego/personality become one, infused with the Divine Love and Wisdom of the Soul. The ego is under the control of the Soul. The lower self is in touch with the Higher Self.

When you become aware of your divine nature – your higher Self – you remember your original state of divinity. This is Plato's Doctrine of Reminiscence. *Gnosis* <u>is</u> the realization of one's own divinity. It's also called Self-Realization – realizing your true nature is your Higher Self. So you see, it's all the same thing. **Know thy Self**

There's nothing inherently wrong with the ego or personality. It's the Soul working in the lower planes. But when the sense mind, under the influence of *Kama*, manipulates the ego into thinking physical "reality" is all there is and all you are is your physical body and personality, your consciousness is very contracted.

When the sense mind (*Manas*) is under control and in tune with the discriminative, harmonious powers of the Soul, it provides a means for the Soul (a unit of Consciousness/Spirit) to express itself in the world of matter as well as the realm of Spirit. You realize you're an immortal soul. Your consciousness is expanded.

This begins to happen when you elevate and expand to soul consciousness. The Soul (Higher Self) guides the ego/personality (lower self). That's why we need to build the "Bridge of Light." The "Bridge of Light" <u>is</u> the Light of the Soul reflecting on the personality.

Don't forget: You don't purify the Soul. You purify the spirit. Your Soul is the "Christ within"/ "Buddha nature."

Part VII

What's Next?

"Turn off your mind, relax and float downstream.
It is not dying, it is not dying.

Lay down all thoughts, surrender to the void.
It is shining, it is shining.

Yet you may see the meaning of within.
It is being, it is being.

Love is all and love is everyone."

"Tomorrow Never Knows"   by Lennon/McCartney

Buddhic Consciousness

So far, we've been focusing on realizing soul consciousness. In soul consciousness, the "Bridge of Light" connects Upper and Lower *Manas*. The Soul is now guiding the personality with *buddhi* intelligence,* discriminative wisdom, and intuition.

Soul consciousness is only the first step. There are higher states of consciousness. Remember the *Buddhic* and *Nirvanic/Atmic* planes? Once you break free of the personality/ego, you can experience these new realms of consciousness. That's where we want to ultimately go.

After soul consciousness – the Soul working through the causal body, the next step is for the Soul to express itself on the *Buddhic* plane through the *Buddhic* body. This is called *Buddhic* consciousness. The predominant quality in the causal body is knowledge, and, ultimately, wisdom. The predominant qualities of consciousness in the *Buddhic* body are **bliss** and **love**.

The *Buddhic* body is called the Bliss sheath (*anandamayakosha*) as well as the spiritual, spirit, or solar, body. To develop the *Buddhic*, or Bliss, body, you must cultivate pure, unselfish, all embracing, and beneficent love. Love that gives everything and asks for nothing in return – Unconditional Love.

Pure love brought the universe into being, pure love maintains it, and pure love draws it upwards towards perfection, towards bliss. **Whenever you pour out love to all who need it, the pure spontaneous joy you experience develops and nurtures the *Buddhic* body.**

On the *Buddhic* plane, there's still duality but there's no separation. **The individual human Soul on the causal plane is merged into the spiritual Soul of unity on the *Buddhic* plane.** There remains a sense of individuality but no feeling of separation from other Souls.

buddhi intelligence is experienced on the causal plane, not to be confused with *Buddhic* consciousness on the *Buddhic* plane.

There's no longer "you" or "me." We're both facets of something which transcends and yet includes "us" both. "I am he as you are he as you are me and we are all together."

The sense of unity is characteristic of the *Buddhic* plane. On that plane, your consciousness expands until you realize/experience the consciousness of your fellows is included within your own, and you feel, know, and experience, with an absolute perfection of sympathy*, all that is in them because it is in reality a part of "your" Self.

Charity and pure love are above all other virtues because by these virtues alone can you participate on the *Buddhic* plane. A selfish person cannot function on the *Buddhic* plane for the essence of that plane is sympathy and compassion, which excludes selfishness.

Turiya, sometimes referred to as the fourth state of consciousness, is related to *Buddhic* consciousness. The other three states of consciousness are waking state, dream state, and dreamless, deep sleep. *Turiya* has been called pure consciousness. The realization of *Turiya* destroys ignorance, desire, attachment, and aversion.

On the *Buddhic* plane, you recognize objects by an entirely different method in which external vibrations play no part. The object becomes part of yourself, and you study it from inside instead of from outside. While the intuition of the causal body recognizes the outer, the intuition of *Buddhi* recognizes the inner.

On the *Buddhic* plane, Consciousnesses don't necessarily merge instantly at the lowest sub-level. They gradually grow wider and wider until the highest level of the *Buddhic* plane is reached. Now, one finds oneself consciously one with all humanity. That's the lowest level at which separateness is absolutely nonexistent. In its fullest, conscious unity with humanity, Creation, and the Divine belongs to the *Atmic/Nirvanic* plane.

*Sympathy doesn't just mean feeling sorry for someone. It's the understanding between people: common feeling, *rapport*, affinity, empathy, harmony, closeness, fellowship, togetherness, communion, friendship

Atmic/Nirvanic Consciousness

The fifth plane, *Nirvanic,* or *Atmic,* is the plane of the highest human aspect of God within us – sometimes called the Self, or *Atma* (Soul)*. On the *Nirvanic* plane, the Soul is pure Spirit without a body. It's the plane of pure existence. What lies beyond on the sixth (*Monadic*) and seventh (*Logoic*) planes is hidden in the unimaginable light of God. Words can't describe it. Minds can't comprehend it.

Atmic, or *Nirvanic,* consciousness, the consciousness belonging to life on the fifth plane, is the consciousness attained by those known as Masters – liberated souls who remain connected with physical bodies for the helping of humanity. They have united the essence of individuality with non-separateness, and live as immortal intelligences, perfect in wisdom, bliss, and power.

Nirvanic consciousness is the antithesis of annihilation. It's existence raised to a vividness and intensity inconceivable to those who know only the life of the senses and the mind. The word *Nirvana* comes from the *Sanskrit* word meaning blown away, blown out, or blown apart – the extinguishing or blowing out of greed, aversion, and illusion.

You realize a state of **non-duality** in *Nirvana.* Your consciousness merges with the consciousness of God. There is no longer you and God. There is only God/Consciousness. You, everyone else, and all of Creation are Consciousness in manifestation Non-duality is experienced as loving, expansive, and blissful unity, lacking any sense of separation. You have a sense of connection with the entire universe. You feel yourself to be whatever you are beholding.

"Thou are That!"

*The Soul has different names on different planes but it always remains a Ray of Divine Light.

The consciousness of love, bliss, and unity on the *Buddhic* plane can be called *Buddhic,* or Christ, Consciousness (depending on your culture) as well as *Salvikalpa Samadhi.* The consciousness of non-duality on the *Nirvanic* plane – *Nirvana* – can also be called *Gnosis*, Self-Realization, and *Nirvikalpa Samadhi*. It's the realization of one's own divinity.

Sun gazing can put you into *Buddhic** and even *Atmic/Nirvanic* consciousness, at least for a while. Behind the process is *Kundalini* rising to the "Spiritual Eye" and Crown *chakras*.

Don't expect it to happen the first time you sun gaze. Just relax and go along for the ride. The more you let go, the more your consciousness elevates and expands. And the more you realize those states of consciousness, the longer you'll be able to maintain them.

*If you can do it by meditation or other spiritual practices, you can do it by sun gazing. Meditation, sun gazing and other spiritual practices can go hand-in-hand.

Note: Christ Consciousness and *Buddhic* Consciousness are the same state of consciousness – no need to change your religious beliefs.

The Shift

Remember Lower *Manas* in the four lower sub-levels of the mental plane and Upper *Manas* in the three upper sub-levels? Lower *Manas* is considered the concrete mind while Upper *Manas* is the abstract mind. Together, they can be thought of as the intellect.*

The intellect is the separative principle in man. It distinguishes between the "I" and the not "I." The intellect is conscious of "itself" and considers everything outside of "itself" as alien. It's the combative, struggling, self assertive principle.

The intellect is the root of all separateness – the source of division and conflict between us. Everyone else's beliefs, thoughts, and opinions are different and apart from yours. This leads to self-interest.

Even when you're in soul consciousness, with upper *Manas* (individual human Soul) controlling lower *Manas* (and the personality/ ego), the Soul still thinks of itself as an individual. **While on the mental and causal planes, with the Soul working through the concrete and abstract minds, you could say your consciousness is intellect-based.**

On the *Buddhic* plane, while the Soul still experiences individuality, it realizes a unity of all Souls. There's no separation. We are all One. **In *Buddhic* consciousness, the Soul is free from the intellect-based mind and personality separating us from other Souls.** When we realize we're all in this together, we'll work for the common good.

Unconditional love and unity are realized when you're consciousness elevates and expands to the *Buddhic* plane. The Soul expresses itself through the heart center in *Buddhic* consciousness. **So, when your consciousness expresses itself through the heart center on the *Buddhic* plane, in unity with all other Souls, you have shifted from intellect-based consciousness to heart-based consciousness.**

*Intellect on the mental plane and intelligence on the causal plane can be regarded together as intellect in this instance because they both refer to the *individual* human "mind."

Shifting from intellect-based consciousness to heart-based consciousness is the next step in our spiritual evolution. It's the hallmark of the New Age of Light.

When we break free from *Kama*/desire and put lower *Manas* in the mental body (personality/ego) under control of upper *Manas* (Soul) in the causal body, moving ourselves into soul consciousness, we call that connection the "Bridge of Light."

In a similar way, the *Buddhic* and astral bodies can be connected. Unconditional love from the *Buddhic* body expresses itself through the astral body* – the body of feelings and emotions. When you realize *Buddhic* consciousness, you could say you've expanded and extended the "Bridge of Light" to unite the *Buddhic* and astral bodies.

Taking it one step further, *Atma*/Self is the pure Soul as Spirit, without any vehicles or "baggage." When you realize *Atmic*/*Nirvanic* consciousness, the Soul expresses itself directly through the Etheric Double and straight to the brain, without having to go through the other bodies where it's vibrations could be diminished by the personality.

That's why *Nirvana* is such an intense, clear, vivid, experience. Totally pure unconditional love, bliss and unity – Oneness. Once again, you've expanded and extended the "Bridge of Light." Somethin' to think about.

*The heart center in particular.

Brotherhood

Individual human souls on the causal plane merge into a consciousness of unity on the *Buddhic* plane. You realize by direct experience humanity is a **Brotherhood** because of the spiritual unity which underlies the *Buddhic* plane. The consciousness of this inner unity, the recognition of the One Self equally in all, is the foundation of Brotherhood.

In *Buddhic* consciousness, there's no loss of individuality, but there is a complete loss of a sense of separation. Your consciousness widens out into a perfect sympathy with the consciousness of others, and you realize you're part of the whole. You don't cease to be yourself. Now, you see yourself as much more.

On the *Buddhic* plane, you **realize** Brotherhood. You see all beings as yourself and feel that what you have is theirs as much as yours. In many cases, more so because their need is greater. You see another's weakness as a call for your help and love. Not an opportunity for you to exploit or take advantage of them. Compassion in the presence of weakness provides patience, tenderness, and protection.

In the New Age of Light, the sense of unity and compassion will be a strength and a power which will be used for service. Strength mandates responsibility and duty. **Understanding, patience, and tolerance are the synthesizing spirit which will characterize the coming New Age of Light.**

Those who recognize the Brotherhood and become conscious within it are able to unite diversity of opinion and character into a common goal – the spiritual evolution of all. They transform diversities into unities, find a place for everyone, and recognize a spiritual unity. Equality, Diversity, Inclusion.

When separateness is abandoned and unity is realized, you find yourself merged with all your brothers and sisters. Your treat everyone with unconditional love.

Not only are you put into harmony with the Masters, but also with those who are still stuck in the lower planes of consciousness. Their feelings must be experienced as well. We're all evolving together.

Some Souls began their journey a long time ago. Others, only more recently. They haven't had time to mature. How can we blame younger Souls who are not yet as highly evolved as we think we, ourselves, are? The word brotherhood suggests an inequality of development, but also the essential unity of all.

In *Buddhic* consciousness, you can easily see things from the other's perspective. You stand in their shoes, and you understand why they're doing what their doing. They're trying to work out their *karma*, just like you are. Whether they know it or not.

You don't have to like what they do. Just don't react to it. Continue to treat them with unconditional love and respect. Hope for the best, even if it doesn't seem to help them. Don't take things personally. The key is not to react to the negativity (detachment). **But do stand up to it.**

You can't expect everyone to think and act the same as you. Even a so-called evil man is part of ourselves. You must pour your strength and love into him, for his benefit, your benefit, and the benefit of all humanity.

The Brotherhood of Humanity has its foundation on the *Buddhic* and *Atmic/Nirvanic* planes, for here alone are unity and perfect sympathy found. This Brotherhood is a spiritual unity already existing as it has since the beginning of Creation. All we have to do is attune to it.

By tuning into the Light of the Solar *Logos* – the Divine Light of which all Souls are rays – we become channels of Its living force. Spiritual Unity is an expression of Divine Love.

The Divinity in you is the same Divinity in me. **<u>We are all rays of the same Divine Light.</u>** The Light in my eyes is the same Light in your eyes – the **"Light of the Soul."**

The "Light of the Soul"

Technically, the Soul doesn't <u>have</u> light. **The Soul is a ray of Divine Light.** Remember: behind our personalities/masks, we are all immortal Souls – "Suns of God." This is our Divine nature – the Divine nature which we all share. When the mask is removed, the "Light of the Soul" shines forth.

The Light shining from a person's eyes is the "Light of the Soul" entering the physical plane, where it meets the light of that plane (physical sunlight) and observes our 3-D physical world. The "Light of the Soul" isn't physical light stored somewhere in the brain. The "Light of the Soul" is the Light of Consciousness/Spirit manifesting on the physical plane through the Soul's vehicles. The eyes **are** the "windows of the Soul."

What happens when a person is dead? There's no longer any Light in their eyes. Where did that Light go? The Soul went back to higher planes, or dimensions of consciousness, to await further incarnations, if necessary, for the subtle body to be purified. More accurately, the "Light of the Soul" doesn't really go anywhere. It just doesn't express itself on the lower planes without it's vehicles.

To reach the brain, vibrations from the Soul in the causal body must pass through the mental and astral bodies. If these bodies are distorted by negative thought-emotion forms and their consequent *samskaras*, they reflect the "Light of the Soul" imperfectly, just as a cracked, dirty mirror will break up and distort images reflected in it.

These negative thoughts-emotion forms will have the effect of stained glass, coloring the "Light of the Soul" and diminishing its Divine radiance.

At the risk of sounding biblical, this is expressed perfectly in *2 Corinthians* 3:18:

"And we, with unveiled faces reflecting like mirrors the brightness of the Lord, all grow brighter and brighter as we are turned into the image that we reflect."

"Unveiled faces" means the mask of the personality has been removed, *i.e.* the spirit has been purified, and we are transformed into "Suns of God."

Isn't that exactly what we do with the Attunement-Reflection Technique? We transform our "faces" by gazing upon the face of God – the Solar *Logos* – to purify our spirits so the "Light of the Soul" can shine forth.

Transfiguration implies an alteration in someone's outward appearance after becoming "enlightened" or "illuminated." When Moses came down from the mountain after conversing with God, his face radiated such a bright light people were afraid of him, even though he was unaware of this Light himself. During the Transfiguration of Jesus, it was said his face "shone like the light of the sun."

Sumerian writings refer to a *melammu* – a blinding "mask of light" radiating from one who has been bestowed Divine Authority. Of the Greek philosopher, Proclus*, it was said his "eyes appeared to be filled with a fulgid** splendor, and the rest of his face to participate in divine illumination."

This radiance is the "Light of the Soul."

Remember: We <u>are</u> "Beings of Divine Light"

*Proclus was one of the last heads of Plato's Academy at Athens before it was destroyed in the 5th century. Proclus prayed to the sun at its rising, its zenith, and its setting.

**shining brightly

"Suns of God"

In most religious art, sacred persons are usually depicted with a Halo in the form of a circle surrounding the head or a circular ring, or disk, above it. Early Halos were represented as an *aura* (from the Latin word: illumination) surrounding the head and are always depicted as though seen full on.

As artists began to paint with perspective (3D), the Halo was portrayed as a ring or flat disk floating above the head or vertically behind it – sometimes as transparent. This disc is sometimes referred to as a Nimbus. Both the Halo and the Nimbus are shown in almost any color or combination of colors but most often appear golden yellow or white.

Other phenomena observed include flames (usually red in color) depicted around the head or the whole body. A *Gloriole* is a crown of light rays meant to resemble the rays of the sun (Statue of Liberty).

A radiant Halo of individual rays is called a Sunburst (like in the symbol of the Solar *Logos*). The whole body image of radiance is sometimes called the *Aureole*, or Glory. It's shown radiating around the body as a luminous golden or white cloud.

What inspired the artists to portray these various symbols of light around religious figures? Some elements, like the *Gloriole* and the Sunburst, are most likely solar symbolism used to make a theological point – a sign of Divinity. But could there be another explanation for the flames, Halo, Nimbus, and *Aureole*? Let's take a look.

It should be noted many people haven't developed the ability to perceive such phenomena. They're not sensitive enough to see the higher vibrations. Their subtle faculties will perceive halos and flames and such, but they're not consciously aware of it.

Their Etheric Double (the connecting link between the subtle body and the physical brain) is not yet developed. Also, few people are so spiritually advanced as to display these phenomena.

If artists weren't clairvoyants, themselves, they had to go with the description of those who could observe the phenomena. Most likely, many artists learned from existing art, not necessarily actually observing these phenomena. What was observed could have been stylized into an artistic tradition – passed on from generation to generation.

The artists were also limited by what they could actually paint on canvas or fashion into a sculpture with the materials and techniques they had available.

On ancient statues of *Buddha* and other Saints, red-orange ray particles are discharged through the top of their heads in the form of a fiery cascade shown as a flame. In *Acts* 2:2, red and yellow flames are said to appear over the heads of the apostles at Pentecost as displayed in paintings.

Remember the splenic *chakra*? It draws in Vitality Globules and breaks the *Prana* into its constituent colors (types of *Prana*). The splenic *chakra* then distributes the appropriate *Prana* to the various force centers. Orange and red *Prana* are sent to the root chakra at the base of the spine. This *Prana* is described as "fiery orange-red."

From the root *chakra*, the orange-red *Prana* flows to the generative organs, energizing the sexual nature. When sexual desire is put aside, this *Prana* is said to go upwards to the brain and the Crown *chakra*. It's involved with the raising of *Kundalini*, which leads to an elevation and expansion of consciousness – "illumination" or "enlightenment." Could this be an explanation for the flames?

When fully awakened, the Crown *chakra* is said to be full of indescribable chromatic effects and vibrates with almost inconceivable rapidity (by those who can perceive it – I can't). On its periphery, it seems to contain all sorts of prismatic hues, but it's predominantly violet. In the center is a whirlpool of gleaming white flushed with gold at the core.

Back to the splenic *chakra*. It also distributes yellow *Prana* to the heart center, which, when developed, is a glowing, golden color. In certain states of consciousness, this *Prana* goes from the heart center to the central core of the Crown *chakra*. Could this be what's become known as a Halo or Nimbus?

The throat *chakra* receives a violet-blue ray of *Prana* from the splenic center. The violet aspect then passes to the outer portion of the Crown *chakra*. Thought and emotion of a high spiritual type are related to the violet ray. Sometimes, violet-blue flames are described above saints.

The Crown center is usually the last to be awakened. Undeveloped, it's the same size as the others. It appears as a depression in the etheric body, like the other *chakras*, because it receives *Prana* from without.

As one progresses spiritually, the Crown *chakra* enlarges until it covers almost the entire top of the head. In a spiritually awakened person, the Crown center reverses itself, turning itself inside out. It's no longer a depression but a dome standing out from the head – a "Crown of Glory," radiating the Solar *Logos*. In statues and paintings of *Buddha*, this crown is portrayed as cascading layers of flames.

What about the *Aureole*, or Glory?* It's been defined as a radiance around the entire body and is shown as a luminous golden or white cloud. Remember Vitality Globules (love that word)? They're *Prana* manifesting in the etheric part of the physical plane. They've been described as brilliant white with a touch of gold.

Consider this. One who absorbs a lot of these Vitality Globules has lots of vitality. If they have more vitality than they can use, this vitality is radiated outwards, where it can be absorbed by others. This radiating vitality could quite possibly give someone a whitish aura several inches around the body edged by gold.

*The word "Glory" is sometimes used to describe the light seen around a spiritual personage.

Remember: Moses and Jesus spent a lot of time in the desert, fasting and praying. That alone would expose them to lots of Vitality Globules. Perhaps they even did a little sun gazing. (Most likely, they did) Could this be what's meant by: "His raiment was as white as snow"?

The causal body is where the individual human Soul resides. The Soul sends its vibrations to the lower planes through the mental, astral, and etheric bodies to the physical body. The causal body of one who has attained a certain level of illumination or enlightenment (an *Arhat*) is referred to as the *Augoeides*, which means "radiant body."

The *Augoeides* of an *Arhat* extends many feet beyond their physical body. It appears delicate and ethereal and at the same time brilliant and luminous. The *Augoeides* has been described as "shining with a sun-like splendor far beyond all imagination in its glorious loveliness. It appears as living fire."

"In the center stands the form of the person appearing as blinding white light surrounded by a golden sphere. Colors are arranged around the physical body in great concentric shells which are penetrated everywhere by radiations of living light, always pouring forth from the person at the center."

Remember: the causal body is the storehouse for the highest and noblest* thoughts and emotions acquired through countless incarnations as the spirit evolves. **When someone has developed this body, they pour forth unconditional love, compassion and sympathy of the highest spirituality, which strengthens the highest qualities of those who come within their presence.**

They shine like the Sun because they've become perfect manifestations of the Solar *Logos*, radiating Divine Love and Wisdom to all those around them. They are **"Suns of God."**

---

*Noble: righteous, virtuous, honorable, honest, good, uncorrupted, ethical, unselfish, generous, self-sacrificing, brave, lofty, exalted, and sublime.

Recap and Commentary

The techniques were presented first so you can start practicing them. After grasping the basics and understanding the proper attitude, which is **extremely** important, it shouldn't take long to get the hang of the Attunement-Reflection Technique. Then, you'll want to incorporate the Crown Technique into your sun gazing routine. The other techniques can be practiced on a need-to basis.

A good grasp of subtle anatomy and the *chakra* system – where spiritual transformation takes place – will help in understanding subtle psychology – what actually happens in spiritual transformation. There's a lot of information packed into those small chapters. Take your time and study them when you can.

The first step is to put the Soul in control of the personality. We call this state soul consciousness. From there, guided by *buddhi* intelligence, discriminative wisdom, and intuition, we can realize the elevated and expanded states of *Buddhic* consciousness and *Atmic/ Nirvanic* consciousness.

That's what we're really headin' for. In those higher states, you go beyond your personality. You realize your unity with all your brothers and sisters and your own essential divinity.

The evolutionary transition into the New Age of Light is founded on the shift of our consciousnesses from intellect-based to heart-based. **This happens when you realize a state of *Buddhic* consciousness. We are the pioneers. The shift begins with us.**

I hope I haven't given the impression the task at hand – spiritual transformation – is easy. What I've presented isn't easy. The Teachings themselves **are** simple. Living them isn't. There's no shortcut to spiritual transformation. You have to go through the process. **The whole point of incarnation is to experience the process. Sun gazing merely accelerates the process.***

*See pgs 173-176

The techniques will work. It depends on how much you're willing and able to devote yourself to practicing them. **It might take some time before you can really get into it on a regular basis. Don't worry about it.** Every time you sun gaze, you'll be gaining ground.

Just because you temporarily realize a state of soul consciousness doesn't mean you're home free. The fun is just beginning. It's an ongoing process, and you'll have challenges. What matters is how you face those challenges

How you live your life. How you treat your fellows. How much Light and Love you can bring into the world. That's what really matters. You don't have to necessarily walk around in deep contemplation 24/7, unless you want to.

The key is to pay attention to how you react to things. How you handle disappointment – not getting your way or what you want. Some people are beautiful rays of sunshine until something doesn't go their way. Then, they turn into bolts of lightning. Don't be like that. **Stay detached.** Observe yourself playing your role in the "movie." Equipoise Equanimity

When people attack you, most likely verbally or psychically, don't get angry. Don't seek revenge or retribution. **Remain detached.** Maintain your highest state – unconditional love. That's your challenge! Don't take things personally. People are going to do what they're going to do. It probably doesn't really have anything to do with you. Develop compassion, unconditional love, tolerance, patience, and understanding.

As you continue to practice sun gazing techniques, your perspective will change. The behavior of others might seem strange to you. Sometimes, your own behavior will seem strange to you. That's good. That means you're starting to progress. Means you're payin' attention.

The key is to not expect everyone else to think like you do. That's part of the game. Try to see things from the other guy's perspective. Remember: we're all in this together. What affects one person, affects everyone.

You must be self observant. It's extremely important to pay attention to your thoughts and emotions. Watch out for selfishness or anything else leading to separation rather than unity. Pay attention to your solar plexus area and heart center.

Eventually, you'll be able to feel "unclean"/aberrant thoughts and emotions. There will be a sharp twinge in the heart center with any thought or emotion that closes the "knot of the heart." Do the "Spirit Cleansing Technique."

Remember:

Be not self centered, but centered in the Self

Be not self critical, but self analytical

Be not self obsessed, but Self aware

You already are your Self

So Be It

Don't forget why you're sun gazing. You want to expand and elevate your consciousness and realize a spiritual transformation. You do this by purifying your spirit/subtle body. Then, *Kundalini* will rise and bring you to higher states of consciousness.

It's the beginning of a New Age of Light – the age of the Soul. The time when we awaken to our true spiritual nature. Our task is to bring more Divine Light, imbued Love and Wisdom, into the world for the evolution/transformation of all of Creation.

Let the Light of your Soul shine forth. Be a living "Sun of God."

Dormant and Latent
Spiritual Faculties

Earlier, I mentioned awakening dormant and latent spiritual faculties. Time to explain what I mean by that. Sun gazing will energize the Etheric Double and the force centers, which will enhance communication between the brain and the astral, mental and causal bodies. This will make you more sensitive to vibrations from the higher planes.

Subtle hearing, called clairaudience, doesn't involve the ears or any other physical organ. The ears only register sound vibrations. It's the subtle body that experiences "hearing."

When the throat *chakra* is awakened, you might hear voices of several different varieties in your mind. Don't freak out! You're not going crazy. You're developing the ability to "hear" on other planes. This can be helpful if you put it into the proper perspective.

If you're unfortunate enough to know someone who's into "mental influence" (black magic), you might be able to hear their malevolent psychic commands or harassment, although the perpetrators are unlikely to know you're aware of what they're doing. Gives you a little edge.

You might also hear voices from people you know, even when they're not around you. This communication happens directly from their mental body to your mental body, meaning they're not necessarily consciously aware of the voices you hear.

Sometimes, their suggestions and comments are helpful. Other times, they're not. The best thing is to pay attention but not necessarily react to what you hear. I've found I usually get positive advice from positive people and negative advice from negative people.

Remember: you're hearing their spirit more than their conscious mind. So, this does give a little insight into what's lurking in their subconscious minds. Just don't get too hung up with it. You'll have to learn how to deal with it.

It's possible you'll hear voices from Beings existing on the higher planes if you're sensitive enough. Whether it be from some poor lost Soul on the astral plane or a more developed Being on the mental or higher planes who's trying to assist you in your evolution. There are also other entities and forces out there. Never a dull moment.

Etheric faculties are extensions of the ordinary physical senses, enabling the possessor to appreciate vibrations pertaining to the etheric portion of the physical plane. As regards to etheric vision, such impressions will be received through the retina of the eye, affecting it's etheric matter.

This might help to explain a phenomenon which I experienced but haven't been able to find any independent information on. Years ago, I noticed some of my friends appearing "animated," like you see in cartoons. They began to look like caricatures of themselves, extending a **few inches** out from their physical bodies.

It seemed I could "see" their mental and emotional states reflected in their faces in a much exaggerated manner. This was pretty startling (and entertaining) at first. I call it "spirit sight" because it seems to involve their mental and emotional bodies, which we've defined as the spirit.

These enhancements of perception will definitely liven up your transformative experience. Don't be expecting them, but don't be surprised if/when they happen. Don't seek these abilities. You could get off track by pursuing occult powers. Psychic faculties will come to you if you need them to help you with your evolution. **Seek soul consciousness and beyond.**

By far, the most important faculties to awaken are those of the Soul. When the personality is put under control of the Soul, you're guided by *buddhi* intelligence, discriminative wisdom, and intuition. If you make use of these new faculties, they will lead you to further spiritual "awakening."

Evolution of the Soul
and *Karma*

Time to explain how sun gazing accelerates your spiritual evolvement and cleans up you *karma*.

When you perform the Attunement-Reflection and Crown Techniques, you're putting yourself in tune with the Solar *Logos* – the expression of Divine Will and the driving and guiding force of our spiritual evolution. Sometimes called *Shakti*, this force can bring about a "quickening" of the spirit.

The purpose of our Soul's "descent" into the lower planes is to learn how to fully express itself in them. We are to become perfect expressions of the Solar *Logos* – "Suns of God." The fact you're even reading this book indicates you're probably an old Soul. One who's been traveling from incarnation to incarnation for a long time.

The Soul's journey takes countless incarnations.* Eventually, you'll evolve to the point where you don't need to incarnate on the lower planes unless you want to return to assist others in their spiritual evolvement. Or you might remain on the higher planes and work from there.

Technically, the Soul doesn't really evolve. It's the Soul's vehicles – the subtle and causal bodies – that need to be developed. When these bodies are perfected, the Soul can fully express itself in the lower planes. This can be called the **"awakening of the Soul."**

You must develop the physical, etheric, and subtle bodies so they can respond to the higher vibrations of the causal plane with its *buddhi* intelligence, discriminative wisdom and intuition, the *Buddhic* plane of bliss and unity, and the *Atmic/Nirvanic* plane of non-duality. This is done by breaking up the negative *samskaras*.

*The doctrine of reincarnation was banned from Christianity in the sixth century. Throughout history, many cultures and religions have embraced the idea of reincarnation. The concept is often grossly misrepresented in the modern Western world.

Samskaras **are the seeds of** *karma** **and** *karma* **is the fruit of** *samskaras.* It all happens in the causal body – home of the human Soul. While the astral and mental bodies eventually disintegrate after an incarnation, the causal body stores the *karma* you've created <u>and</u> the **virtues** you've developed. The level of consciousness you realize in an incarnation is recorded here.

In the next incarnation, the causal body lays out the blueprint for the makeup of the lower vehicles according to your past positive and negative *samskaras* <u>and</u> your accumulated *karma*** – the net result of your past actions. You pick up where you left off. Unless, you lived a really bad life the last time, intentionally exhibiting an inordinate amount of selfishness and cruelty. This can lead to a "negation of spirit." Could set you back a bit.

Divine Will is Love and Unity. Divine Will is the force behind our spiritual evolution. In fact, it's behind the evolution of all Creation. **Any action opposing your spiritual evolution, or anyone else's, is a breach of that Will. Bad** *karma* **is a result of these negative actions. The negative actions are caused by negative** *samskara***<u>s</u>.**

That's how *samskaras* and *karma* are related. The word, *karma*, literally <u>means</u> thought, action, and deed. Positive *samskaras* (positive thought-emotion forms) lead to good thoughts and actions which create good *karma*. Negative *samskaras* (negative thought-emotion forms) are at the root of your bad action. They cause you to accumulate negative *karma*, which has to be cleared in this lifetime or is carried over to your <u>next</u> life.

* Like reincarnation, the concept of *karma* is often misunderstood, but that's way beyond the scope of this book. I'm only trying to relate *karma* with sun gazing and spiritual transformation.

** In this case, you **<u>do</u>** take it with you. (humor)

When you break up the negative *samskaras* and replace them with positive *samskaras*, you can clean up your *karma*. You free yourself from the negative *samskaras* that led to your past bad behavior and cultivate positives *samaskaras* that will lead to appropriate actions and deeds in the future. *That's how sun gazing can accelerate your evolution – by replacing negative thought-emotion forms with positive ones.*

Karma is not just a simple "punishment and reward" deal." **Your present *karma* puts you in the position to make the right decisions for you to clean up your past bad *karma*. It's like a wake up call.**

Karma doesn't make the decisions for you. It's **your** free will to make the right choice, or the wrong one. **You have the opportunity to create good *karma* by performing right actions and deeds to counteract your previous wrong actions and deeds. Sometimes, this opportunity arises quickly in one's life. Other times, it could take one or more future incarnations.**

Karma is trying to teach you a lesson. The lessons you need to learn to behave properly for the elevation and uplifting of humanity. **The whole idea is to advance your and everyone else's spiritual evolution. From separateness to Unity. It's your thoughts, actions, and deeds that affect this evolution.**

The way you do this is by replacing negative *samskaras* with positive *samskaras* and elevating and expanding your consciousness. You move closer to Unconditional Love and Unity and the realization of your and everyone else's Divinity. You can do this by sun gazing which attunes you to Divine Will. **Divine Will wants you to evolve.**

When in tune with the *Shakti*/Divine Will, the principle of synchronicity is enhanced. Everything happens for a reason. You realize every situation is an opportunity to evolve. An opportunity for you to make the right call. The right move. *

*When you're guided by the *buddhi* intelligence, discriminative wisdom, and intuition of the Soul, you're led to making the right actions.

You become a magnet for challenging situations. That's how your evolution is accelerated. So, follow your intuition. Surrender to the *Shakti*. Learn your lessons. Accept what's happening and make the best of it. If you make the right choices, bad *karma* is cleared out. You make the wrong ones, it's back to school. You get as many do-overs as it takes – the purpose/meaning of reincarnation.

Life's supposed to be a challenge. That's what you're here for. That's how you learn. Do the right thing in a bad situation. If things are going too easy, you won't be forced to grow, to evolve. Embrace the challenge. Savor it. Hold on tight and ride out the storm. Enjoy yourself. **The key is to remain detached.** Look at your life as a role in an adventure movie. A *karmic* movie.

Let Divine Will play out. Don't take yourself too seriously. Don't take things personally. Don't respond to the negativity. Don't get angry. Don't seek revenge. Maintain your state of equanimity and equipoise. Don't let things bother you. That way, your consciousness won't contract when things go wrong. You'll be at your best.

The goal is to purify the spirit of all selfish thoughts and emotions contracting your consciousness. **All the while, developing the elevating and expanding qualities/virtues of selflessness, compassion, sympathy, and unconditional love.** Restructuring your personality takes time.

When you're conscious on the causal, *Buddhic*, and *Atmic/Nirvanic* planes, you're replacing consciousness contracting vibrations (thoughts and emotions) with consciousness expanding vibrations. You could call this raising your vibrational rate, or elevating your frequency. The goal is to make this higher state permanent.

You want to attune to the ultimate frequency/vibration – Divine Love. Then, you become a **"Sun of God."**

It all starts with how you treat others.
Try a little kindness!

Recommended Bibliography

The books listed below have been very helpful to me. I used some of the ideas expressed in these references to offer an explanation for how sun gazing can bring about a spiritual transformation.

In no way am I suggesting any of these authors would agree as to how I used their ideas. (Hopefully, they would) I'm also not claiming I'm representing their teachings. I didn't use direct quotes because I'm not using their teachings to validate mine. Only to help explain my ideas.

Admittedly, I've taken things out of context and patched them together to make <u>my</u> point which might not necessarily be the same as what the authors originally intended. As far as I know, none of these authors practiced, taught, or promoted sun gazing.

Spiritual transformation is spiritual transformation. Elevating and expanding consciousness is elevating and expanding consciousness. Purifying the *Nadis* and the subtle body is purifying the *Nadis* and the subtle body. Loosening the "knot of the heart" is loosening the "knot of the heart." *Kundalini* rising is *Kundalini* rising.

It doesn't matter how you go about it. Sun gazing is one way – a seemingly much quicker way.

God Talks With Arjuna The Bhagavad Gita   *Paramahansa Yogananda*

The Chakras   Charles Leadbeater

Man Invisible and Invisible   "

The Ancient Wisdom   Annie Besant   – great introductory overview

Man and His Bodies   "

The Seven Principles in Man   "

Thought-Forms   Beasant & Leadbeater

The Etheric Double   A.E. Powell

The Astral Body   "

The Mental Body   "

The Causal Body and the Ego   "

The Doctrine of the Subtle Body in Western Tradition   GRS Mead

The Chakras and the Human Energy Fields   *Shafica Karagulla* M.D.

The Serpent Fire   Raymond Bernard

The Primal Power in Man or the Kundalini Shakti   *Swami Narayanananda*

Foundations of Tibetan Mysticism   *Lama Anagarika Govinda*

Is Ultimate Reality Unlimited Love?   Stephen G. Post

Informative websites: the following websites offer great insight into what's happening to the world on the subtle level. The **"Big Picture."** Totally awesome stuff!

whenthesoulawakens.org   they offer a free PDF: *Entering the Age of Light*

callfromthemountain.net   they offer several free PDF's

While not mentioned in the text, *The Four Agreements* by Miguel Ruiz offers some **excellent** practical advice on how to deal with life while on your path.

Spiritual Vibrational Healing

Here's a technique for opening the heart center <u>and</u> elevating and expanding consciousness that doesn't necessarily involve sun gazing. You could call it spiritual vibrational healing because you're healing the spirit with vibration.

By chanting vowel sounds at specific frequencies, the force centers in the subtle and etheric bodies can be activated and put into balance, allowing optimum energy flow. This helps put you in a state of elevated and expanded consciousness, at least for a while. Of course, the goal is to ultimately maintain the expanded and elevated state permanently.

To put it another way, you can attune yourself to the Divine Love and Wisdom emanating from the Solar *Logos*. On a more down to earth level, the simple act of rhythmically chanting the different frequencies stills the mind and calms the emotions, putting you into a meditative state. This also expands and elevates your consciousness.

Review: *Chakras*/force centers are energy centers, or portals, in the subtle body. They originate at various centers along the astral spine (*Sushumna*) of the body from the base of the spine to the top of the head. They're whirling vortices through which Creative Intelligent Life Force (*Prana*) flows in and out of the etheric and subtle bodies.

Energy flows through the *chakra* system in two ways. First, it flows up and down along the central channel (*Sushumna*, subtle spine) connecting the *chakras*. Second, it flows horizontally in the exchange of energy with the Cosmos through the *chakras*.

Chakras can be over or under active, or become blocked or imbalanced, all which interfere with energy flow. Unblocking the force centers can elevate consciousness. Tuning the centers puts them in harmony with the *Logos*, enhances communication between the subtle body, the Etheric Double, and the physical body, <u>and</u> expands and elevates one's consciousness by allowing *Kundalini* to rise.

We'll be working with the eight major *chakra* system I discussed earlier. These force centers of energy exchange originate in the subtle spinal centers, medulla, and cerebrum. They're associated with various nerve plexuses, the brain stem, and the brain, and are sometimes related to various endocrine glands and organs.

For reasons I can't adequately explain, the force centers are also related to frequencies corresponding to the notes of the major scale in the key of C, as well as to colors.

I just accept it and work with it. And it **does** work! I know because I can feel my force centers vibrating/resonating when performing this technique.

Fortunately for me, and perhaps you as well, this technique requires no singing ability. You slowly chant a word/sound while maintaining the same pitch. There's no need to be loud. You're not projecting your voice outward. You're trying to create an <u>internal</u> vibration.

Soft and gentle. You don't have to belt it out. You not trying to break a glass or a window. You can even hum quietly, as long as you feel a vibration.

Sit comfortably in a chair, with your spine straight. You can also do this technique standing up, as long as you're comfortable.

Take a few slow, deep breaths to relax and center yourself.

To begin, draw in a deep breath. There's no need to strain to completely fill your lungs with air. As you practice, your lung capacity will increase.

Pause for a moment, holding your breath.

Begin with middle C (the lower C note on a pitch pipe in the key of C) for the root/coccygeal center. A keyboard is also handy. If you're using a guitar, start with the C on the first fret of the B string. Slowly and smoothly vocalize *do* in the proper pitch (middle C) until you run out of breath.

Feel for a vibration in the root center <u>while</u> you're chanting. This is the important part – creating a resonance within you. If you don't have access to a pitch pipe or other musical source, experiment. Try chanting a sound and notice where you feel resonance.

Then work from there – raising or lowering the pitch of your chant to connect with the various *chakras*. You'll know it when you feel it. It might take a little practice. Be patient! It's easier if you have a pitch pipe.

Wait a few seconds – 5 to 10, or longer, if you wish – and repeat the same note again. Try several times if you like, each time concentrating on the feeling in the coccygeal/root center.

Remember: the centers are along the midline of your torso on the front surface of your etheric and physical bodies and at the top of your head. That's where you'll probably feel the resonance – a subtle vibration. You might feel it closer to your spine.

Don't worry if you can't feel anything at first. Just keep practicing. You're shakin' things up. The technique will still elevate your consciousness.

Slowly work through the rest of the *chakras* – sacral (D – *re*), solar plexus (E – *mi*), splenic *chakra* (F – *fa*), heart center (G – *sol*), throat/cervical (A – *la*), brow/"Spiritual Eye"/medulla (B – *ti*), finally ending with the Crown *chakra* (C – *do* an octave higher than the root *chakra*) at the top of the head.

Some *chakra* systems differ slightly, but that's not really important. The point is to go through the octave, ascending from middle C at the root *chakra* to the Crown *chakra*, feeling the vibration in each center along the way.

You might try visualizing the corresponding color of each *chakra* as you're attuning to it. This will reinforce the frequency of the vibration you're creating. **Note:** there are several different color systems taught. Just use the one you're comfortable with. The important thing is the "feeling" you get when chanting. Go through the octave! **See Diagram 3**

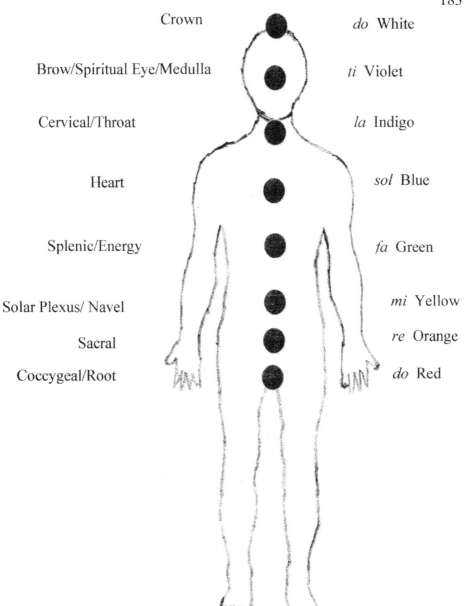

Crown — *do* White

Brow/Spiritual Eye/Medulla — *ti* Violet

Cervical/Throat — *la* Indigo

Heart — *sol* Blue

Splenic/Energy — *fa* Green

Solar Plexus/ Navel — *mi* Yellow

Sacral — *re* Orange

Coccygeal/Root — *do* Red

CHAKRA/FORCE CENTER SYSTEM

Sound and Color Chart

Diagram 3

After you get the hang of it, you can get a little more specific with your chant. Instead of using the do re mi's, try chanting *AUM* at the various frequencies. Here's why:

Absolute Spirit manifests in Creation as a Cosmic Vibration which expresses Itself as Cosmic Sound <u>and</u> Cosmic Light. Called the *Udghita* by the ancient Brahman priests of India, *OM* is the first expression of God in the Universe.

OM is that Cosmic Sound – the <u>sound</u> of the Solar *Logos* (Love is the emotion/feeling). *AUM* is the verbalization of *Om*. 'O' is a combination of 'A' and 'U'. In Christian terminology, this vibration is known as the Word and called the *Pranava* by the Hindus.

When in tune, the force centers emanate the sound of *AUM*. Each center has a variation (different frequency) of the cosmic sound, starting with middle C at the root/coccygeal center and ascending the major scale, note by note, to complete the octave at the crown center, or slightly above it.

Unfortunately, they're often out of tune, which results in energy blockage. By chanting *AUM*, you can harmonize the centers to the *OM* vibration, allowing the energy to flow properly. And you'll be in tune with the "Song of the *Logos*."

There are various ways to pronounce the *AUM*/Amen (Christian)/Ameen (Islamic) vibration. The way I was taught seems to work quite well.* Here it is:

<u>**Ah Oh OOO (like in moon) Meh (like in men) Neh (like in never) Meh eN**</u>

* A simple *OM* or *AUM* will work fine. Or, use the do re mi's if you like.

After drawing in a deep breath, slowly pronounce each syllable as you breathe out, running them together as you chant so it sounds like you're saying one word in slow motion. You're basically saying the word like you normally would, only "stretching" it out. Work on that for a while.

As you develop your chanting ability, you might want to try this: slowly exhale while pronouncing:

Ah Ah Ah Oh Oh Oh OOO OOO OOO Meh eh eh Neh eh eh Meh eh eh eN n n

Once again, like you're saying the word in slow-motion with a pulsating rhythm. It's almost like an echo or a tremolo effect. You might have to take more than one breath to get through it. That's fine. I do.

Notice that by going through the sounds, starting with ah, then oh, ooo, meh, and en, you can feel the sound moving from the back of your oral cavity (mouth) forward as you slowly close your mouth/lips when saying meh, finally with your tongue resting on your teeth as you pronounce en. Repeating the meh and en reinforces the vibration.

Try doing this several times for each force center, working your way through the octave. Take your time. Get into it. Keep the syllables connected as you pronounce them. Don't make it choppy or abrupt. Slow, continuous, and smooth is the ticket.

Pronouncing *AUM* in this matter produces a rolling, pulsating vibration causing the center to vibrate in the same manner (sympathetic vibration), thus attuning it to the *OM* at the corresponding frequency.

This restores the center to balance, puts it into harmony with the *OM,* and corrects an under or overactive *chakra*. This opens the *chakra* and allows proper energy exchange which enlivens and illuminates it. It sorta rocks you into tune. You might have to draw more than one breath to get through the whole word. That's okay. Take as many as you need.

Here's a thought. Once you feel comfortable going through the octave chanting *AUM*, **try doing it while sun gazing! The results will be amazing!** 1-3x for each force center is enough unless you feel the need for more. Usually, I focus on the heart, throat, brow, and Crown *chakras*.

Harmonize the force centers with the Solar *Logos*. Correct under and over activity. Allow energy to flow properly. Elevate your conscious awareness to the higher centers. Expand your consciousness to higher dimensions.

That's what you're shootin' for. It happens automatically. You'll notice the difference. I first practiced this technique with a group and almost went straight through the ceiling!

Try It! It works.

Note to Sun Gazers

That's all for now. Part 2 of *The "Mysteries of the Light"* will eventually be forthcoming. It will discuss the nature of the Spiritual Sun, Light, the physical sun, the etheric plane, and a few other topics.

<u>Relax.</u> Fear not! You already have all the techniques and background information you need for spiritual transformation by sun gazing and experiencing higher states of consciousness. Get to Work!!!

Abbreviated Techniques

For your convenience, I've condensed the techniques into simplified instructions. You can easily remove these pages from the book, or you could make copies of them so you won't have to take the entire book with you when you go to practice them. If you're not sure about something, you can always refer to the book.

Attunement-Reflection Technique

Perform the technique at sunrise and/or sunset. You can start the technique shortly before the sun comes up. At sunset, begin when you're able.

Stand, or sit, in a comfortable position so you're relaxed. If possible, hold your arms out in front of you so your palms are facing the sun. Or let them hang down at your sides with your palms facing the sun. Use a cross in your left hand facing the sun if you want to.

Still the mind and calm the emotions. **Very important!**

Breathe slowly and steadily.

Relax! You're surrendering to God's Divine Will and reflecting His Love. If you relax, you'll attune with the Light. It's a natural process. You're not really trying to do anything. It's an entirely passive act.

You don't need to focus directly on the solar sphere. Relax your vision. Try gently looking at the tip or bridge of your nose, with your eyes at half mast. Remember. You're looking at the Light, not the solar orb.

Face the sun. Gaze from right to left and back a few times, up and down, as well as diagonally. Rotate your head slightly rather than just moving you're eyes, if you like. Look around the sun in a slow circular manner – either clockwise, or counterclockwise, gazing off to the side of the sun all the way around, once again moving your head a little bit. Experiment. Just keep it movin'.

As you sun gaze, blink at a slow rate, faster if you like. Get into a rhythm.

Don't focus on the sun. Look for the Light within the light.

Remember why you're sun gazing. You're attuning to God's Light and Love. You're elevating and expanding your consciousness. Open up to your higher Self and enter a state of Unconditional Love. You're now a mirror reflecting God's Light and Love to all Creation.

Please refer to pg 25 for an expanded explanation, if you need to.

Crown Technique

After sun gazing for a few minutes to get in tune/warmed up with the Attunement-Reflection Technique, while still holding your left palm with your cross facing the sun, take your right palm and place it over the top of your head (the Crown *chakra*), perhaps a quarter inch or half inch above it.

Five minutes should be long enough, but feel free to go longer if you like. If your right arm gets tired, just lower it for a moment or two to loosen up and then place it back over your head. When you're done, continue with the Attunement-Reflection Technique for awhile if you like.

You can also do this technique over your heart chakra, "Spiritual Eye," or whatever other *chakra* you want. I believe the Crown and the heart are the most important – they work together.

You **could** say you're anointing your Crown *chakra* with the Solar *Logos* because **that's what you're doing.**

Important! **As you perform the Crown Technique, continue doing the basic Attunement-Reflection procedure – moving your gaze around while blinking in a slow rhythmic beat and gently directing your gaze to the spot on your forehead between your eyes with your eyes at half mast.**

When you're finished doing the Crown Technique, continue with the Attunement-Reflection Technique for a while if you like.

Please refer to pg. 35 for a complete description

Heart Center Technique

While performing the Attunement-Reflection Technique, with your cross in your left hand facing the sun, place your right hand over your heart *chakra,* about a quarter inch away from your body.

Remember to continue sun gazing in the previously prescribed manner. This technique will attune the heart center with the expression, or feeling, of the Solar *Logos* – Divine Love.

Concentrate your awareness on the heart center as you perform the technique. Feel the love pouring into you and filling your entire being.

After a time, a few minutes or more, take your right palm and face it towards the sun with your left hand and cross still facing the sun. This will close the circuit with the Spiritual Sun.

Feel the love radiating to everyone and everything. You have an endless supply of this Divine Love, because it's your true nature.

Experience Unity with all of Creation and the Creator. **Be the Love. Feel the Bliss. When you feel these qualities, you radiate them outwards spontaneously. You're a channel of Divine Love.**

You can make it a meditation if you like. Envision the Divine Love emanating from you and surrounding and enveloping everything and everyone around you. You **are** the Light (imbued with Divine Love), so **Be** the Light.

It doesn't need to be sunny. You can perform this technique when it's overcast. Just gaze where you think the sun is and go for it. You'll probably be able to see <u>some</u> Light. Perhaps, of a soft golden hue. Notice the warmth in your heart center.

You're centered in your heart *chakra* – the center of your being.

You're calm, peaceful, and serene. At one with everything and everyone. You're in your highest state – **Unconditional Love.**

See pg 39 for full description

Spirit Cleansing Technique

If you ever feel spiritually "unclean," try this technique, preferably on a sunny day:

Sit down outside on a chair, a boulder, or some steps with your bare feet on a flat rock, concrete, or some grass. This will ground you. Plain dirt might get a little muddy. You can glance up at the sun occasionally while you perform this technique.

Take a little time. Relax. Get into it. Pour, or splash with your fingers, a small amount (ounce or so) of <u>cold (more shock value)</u> water over each foot. Wait a few seconds and do it again. Wait a moment and do it one more time for a total of 3x. Remember: you're not bathing.

Next, wash your hands slowly three times with the cold water, pausing briefly between each wash. Don't rush things. Savor the experience. Observe how you feel. <u>You don't need a whole lot of water.</u>

After that, pour a little cold water on your fingertips and splash/ rub it on your forehead – 3 times of course. Just a few drops

Do the same thing to the nape of your neck. Just a few drops, once again. 3x

Finally, to the top of your sternum, if you care to. Yep, 3x, just a few drops.

You'll probably feel more relaxed now – more centered. Your breathing will be deeper. You'll be more open to the Light.

Take an inventory of your thoughts and emotions. See if you still feel any negativity. Hopefully, you won't. At least for a while.

If you have any sacred stones or a cross you use during sun gazing, you can rinse them 3x and hold them up to the sun to purify them. You might even notice the Light of the Sun will now seem more pure.

No need to do this technique every day. Only when you feel like you need it. Think of it as a quick tuneup.   See pg 41 for full explanation

Spiritual Vibrational Healing Technique

Sit comfortably in a chair with your spine straight. Take a few slow, deep breaths to relax and center yourself. To begin, draw in a deep breath.

Begin with middle C for the root/coccygeal (*red*) center. Slowly and smoothly vocalize *do* in the proper pitch (middle C) until you run out of breath. Feel for a gentle vibration in the root center. This is the important part – creating a resonance within you.

Wait a few seconds – 5 to 10 or longer if you wish, and repeat the same note again. Try several times if you like, each time concentrating on the feeling in the coccygeal/root center.

Slowly work through the rest of the *chakras* – sacral (D – *re/orange*), solar plexus (E – *mi/yellow*), splenic center (F – *fa/green*), heart center (G – *sol/blue*), throat/cervical (A – *la/indigo*), brow/"Spiritual Eye"/medulla (B – *ti/violet*), finally ending with the Crown *chakra* (C – *do/white*) an octave higher than the root *chakra*) at the top of your head. Try visualizing the corresponding color of each *chakra* as you're attuning to it.

When you're ready, try the *AUM*. Slowly pronounce each syllable as you breathe out, running them together as you chant so it sounds like you're saying one word in slow-motion. Go through the scale. Repeat as you wish. A simple *OM* or *Aum* is okay. Or try the way I learned:

Ah Oh OOO (like in moon) Meh (like in men) Neh (like in never) Meh eN   or perhaps:

Ah Ah Ah Oh Oh Oh OOO OOO OOO Meh eh eh Neh eh eh Meh eh eh eN n n

Make it a slow, pulsating, continuous chant. Always feel for the resonance in the appropriate center. Take an extra breath if you need to in order to pronounce it. Repeat for each force center as you wish.

Try the routine while sun gazing. Try concentrating on the heart center.

Refer to pg 179 for the full explanation.

Printed in Great Britain
by Amazon

27049522R00126